DATE DUE

q			
Vol.			
201-6503			Printed in USA

DODD, MEAD WONDERS BOOKS include WONDERS OF:

ALLIGATORS AND CROCODILES.
   Blassingame
ANIMAL NURSERIES. Berrill
BARNACLES. Ross and Emerson
BAT WORLD. Lavine
BEYOND THE SOLAR SYSTEM.
   Feravolo
BISON WORLD. Lavine and Scuro
CACTUS WORLD. Lavine
CAMELS. Lavine
CARIBOU. Rearden
CORALS AND CORAL REEFS.
   Jacobson and Franz
CROWS. Blassingame
DINOSAUR WORLD. Matthews
DONKEYS. Lavine and Scuro
EAGLE WORLD. Lavine
ELEPHANTS. Lavine and Scuro
FLY WORLD. Lavine
FROGS AND TOADS. Blassingame
GEESE AND SWANS. Fegely
GEMS. Pearl
GOATS. Lavine and Scuro
GRAVITY. Feravolo
HAWK WORLD. Lavine
HERBS. Lavine
HOW ANIMALS LEARN. Berrill
HUMMINGBIRDS. Simon
JELLYFISH. Jacobson and Franz
KELP FOREST. Brown
LLAMAS. Perry
LIONS. Schaller
MARSUPIALS. Lavine

MEASUREMENT. Lieberg
MONKEY WORLD. Berrill
MOSQUITO WORLD. Ault
OWL WORLD. Lavine
PELICAN WORLD. Cook and Schreiber
PONIES. Lavine and Casey
PRAIRIE DOGS. Chace
PRONGHORN. Chace
RACCOONS. Blassingame
RATTLESNAKES. Chace
ROCKS AND MINERALS. Pearl
SEA GULLS. Schreiber
SEA HORSES. Brown
SEALS AND SEA LIONS. Brown
SNAILS AND SLUGS. Jacobson and
   Franz
SPIDER WORLD. Lavine
SPONGES. Jacobson and Pang
STARFISH. Jacobson and Emerson
STORKS. Kahl
TERNS. Schreiber
TERRARIUMS. Lavine
TREE WORLD. Cosgrove
TURTLE WORLD. Blassingame
WILD DUCKS. Fegely
WOODS AND DESERT AT NIGHT. Berrill
WORLD OF THE ALBATROSS. Fisher
WORLD OF BEARS. Bailey
WORLD OF HORSES. Lavine and Casey
WORLD OF SHELLS. Jacobson and
   Emerson
WORLD OF WOLVES. Berrill
YOUR SENSES. Cosgrove

Wonders of
Snails & Slugs

MORRIS K. JACOBSON & DAVID R. FRANZ

Illustrated with photographs and line drawings

DODD, MEAD & COMPANY
NEW YORK

To Andrew—D.F.

PICTURE CREDITS: R. Tucker Abbott, pages 49, 50; American Museum of Natural History, pages 6, 8, 9, 12, 33, 59, 62, 86; Wayne Aspey, page 71; Frank C. Baker, page 43; Ray S. Bassler, page 53; Kerry Clark, page 26, 77, 78; William Clench and Yoshio Kondo, page 37; Paul Fischer, pages 24, 42; David R. Franz, frontispiece, pages 16, 20, 21, 22, 36, 45, 64, 68, 69, 73, 82; C. S. Lipton and J. Murray, page 58; A. R. Mead, page 61; J. Pearce and G. Thorson, pages 34, 35; G. T. Peterson (from Mead), page 60; G. Raeihle, pages 11, 24; Alan Solem, page 29, 54.

FRONTISPIECE: *Top view of freshwater tadpole snail. The white spots are on the mantle, which can be seen through the transparent shell.*

EP1932 594.35

Copyright © 1980 by Morris K. Jacobson and David R. Franz
Printed in the United States of America

1 2 3 4 5 6 7 8 9 10

LIBRARY OF CONGRESS CATALOGING IN PUBLICATION DATA

Jacobson, Morris K
    Wonders of snails and slugs.

    Bibliography: p.
    Includes index.
    SUMMARY: Discusses the characteristics and
behavior of a variety of snails and slugs and their
uses by man.
    1. Snails—Juvenile literature.   [1. Snails]
I. Franz, David R., joint author.   II. Title.
QL430.4.J32   594′.3   79-6646
ISBN 0-396-07810-9

Contents

A mass of colorful Cuban land snail shells, all one kind in spite of the variety of patterns.

1

Introducing Snails & Slugs

The French call them *escargots* and eat them with flavored butter as a delicacy. Italians call them *maruzze* and mix them with spaghetti sauce. In Germany they are called *Schnecken*, and Catholic peasants often eat them during Lent, when meat is forbidden. In Spain and Portugal, where they are called *caracoles*, they are cooked in a casserole of garlic, olive oil, vegetables, and spices.

The creature that is cooked in these various fancy ways is simply the ordinary land snail, the little animal that walks on its stomach, builds and carries its "house" on its back, has two cute "horns" on its head, and leaves a fine silvery trail on garden walks and pavements over which it has passed.

The snail's most familiar feature is its shell. Some snail shells reach a diameter of sixty centimeters (about two feet); others are so small they have to be examined under a microscope. Marine snails, snails that live in the oceans, form the largest and most showy shells among all snails. Snails that live in fresh water and on land form handsome shells, too, but rarely are they as beautiful as those from the sea.

Some people take such an avid interest in snail shells that they collect shells from all over the world, often paying high

Shells of several species of poisonous cone snails. These are highly prized by collectors.

prices for rare and beautiful specimens. Most museums of natural history also maintain large collections of strange, handsome shells for the delight of visitors and for use by shell students. Although marine snail shells are the most actively sought, on account of their size and beauty, many people who collect shells, and especially collectors for museums, seek both land and freshwater snail shells. Snail shells without the snails inside can be found in large numbers on ocean beaches, on river banks, and on lake shores. There are also many snail shells in forests, parks, and empty city lots. But you have to look carefully for such shells, because most of these are usually dull in color—like the ground on which they rest—and many are no bigger than the head of a pin.

Snail shells have become increasingly popular as personal ornaments, and are often used in necklaces, brooches, and earrings. Some people think shells can be just as beautiful as more expensive jewelry.

Zoologists who specialize in the study of shells are called *conchologists*, and those who study the snail inside, as well as its shell, are called *malacologists*. "Malacologist" comes from the Greek word for "soft," because the body of the snail inside the shell is soft. Today, most people who study snails professionally are malacologists.

But a shell is simply the hard outer skeleton of the soft-bodied snail. Just as we humans unwittingly grow our own inner skeletons of hard bone, so snails grow their hard outer skeletons of shell material. There are glands in the bodies of all sorts of animals—including human beings—that can extract calcium, or lime, from the food they eat and the water they drink, and using other materials, turn them into bones or shells. When the snail that forms the shell dies, the soft body disappears but the empty shell is left.

An accumulation of brackish water snail shells found during the dry season on a lagoon bottom.

What are snails? Snails are part of a large group of animals that have soft bodies without any internal hard parts. Clams, oysters, octopuses, and squids are among the other animals in this group. Since all these animals have soft bodies, and the Latin word for soft is *mollis*, they are called *mollusks*. This kind of large group of related animals is called a *phylum* by zoologists. Hence the phylum of soft-bodied animals, most of which form shells, is called the phylum *Mollusca*. Mollusca is just the formal, scientific expression for mollusks. Zoologists divide a phylum into smaller groups of more closely related animals. These they call *classes*, and to each class they give a name that in some way fits its members. Zoologists noted that snails seem to walk on their stomachs, that their stomachs seem to be their feet. Therefore, a French zoologist decided to call snails *gastropods* (Gastropoda, in formal language), a word that means "stomach-foot." The name stuck. The word is made up of two Greek words: *gastro*, meaning "stomach" (also found in the word gastritis, an inflammation of the stomach), and *poda*, meaning "foot," (as in the words podiatrist, a foot doctor, and podium, a place where a speaker stands). Other groups of mollusks were assigned to different classes and given their own descriptive names. Octopuses and squids, which seem to have their "feet," or tentacles, growing from their heads, were called *cephalopods* (Cephalopoda) because *cephalo* means "head" in Greek. Clams and oysters and their relatives are in the class *Bivalvia* because they have two (*bi* as in bicycle, two wheels) shells, or valves (*valvia* in Latin).

In all, there are seven classes of mollusks, but the gastropods, or snails, are by far the largest class. In fact, there are more kinds, or species, of gastropods known than there are in all the other six classes of mollusks combined.

Most gastropods form outer shells, but some do not, and these are called slugs. Although the slugs that are most familiar

10

A *dorsal view of a marine snail. The extended foot can be totally withdrawn into the shell. Note the eyes at the base of the tentacles and the siphon between.*

11

to us are found on land, a greater number live in the sea. Both land and sea slugs are mollusks, but otherwise, they are not too closely related. No slugs, however, live in fresh water.

Scientists wonder where the mollusks, including the gastropods, came from: from what group of animals are they descended? Many different answers have been offered, but most

A sea slug.

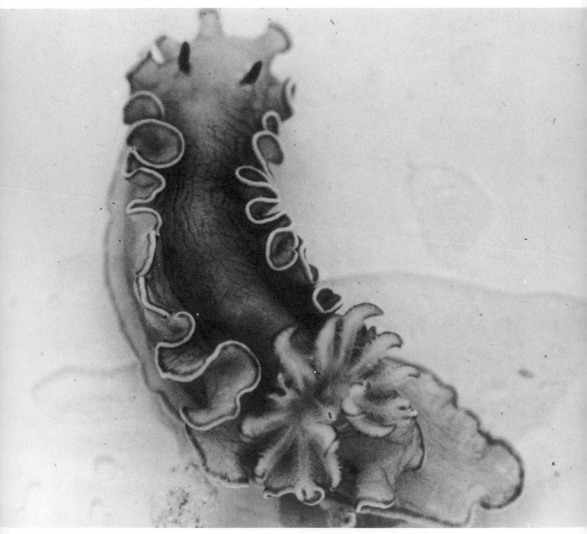

zoologists now believe that mollusks descend from an animal that was an ancestor of both flatworms and mollusks. Flatworms, so to speak, are the cousins of mollusks. There are several reasons for this idea, but perhaps the simplest one is that a large flatworm, for all its differences, does look a good deal like a very flat slug. It is not likely that the gastropods were the first class of mollusks to appear, but whenever zoologists draw pictures of what they believe to be the original mollusk, it looks very much like a limpet without its shell. (A limpet is a snail with a shell that looks like a Chinese peasant hat or a small pointed cup.) The way in which such a creature gave rise to the seven classes of mollusks is not fully understood. But however the mollusks appeared, they have developed into a very successful group of animals. Only the huge army of insects has more species than the mollusks. And, most mollusks are gastropods.

2
Snails, Slugs, & Mankind

Like many animals, snails often show up in our beliefs, our myths, and our legends.

What is the first thing that comes to your mind when you hear the word snail? Most likely it is the idea of slow movement. "Slow as a snail" or "a snail's pace" are expressions found in almost every language in the world. Snails are even slower than tortoises. As a joke, people in the New York City area refer to an unreliable commuter railroad as a "snailroad." And yet, snail races are not unheard of. People have been known to draw a circle on a table, put a number of snails in the center, and then bet. The first snail to reach the edge of the circle wins. But for this sort of game, a great deal of patience is needed. You can't prod a snail to move faster, because if you do, it just flashes back into its shell and stays there until it is good and ready to come out. You have to let snails take their own sweet time. And that can be long!

Another idea people associate with snails is lowliness in rank and style of living. A well-known song has the line "I'd rather be a sparrow than a snail." The sparrow, like most birds, represents energy, joy, music, song, hope. Snails represent humbleness, gloom, patience, even boredom. This is not to say that birds and snails really have these attributes; rather, this is how some people look upon them.

Snails are often also associated with snugness and shelter. A snail always carries its house around with it, like a mobile home. The "house" is the shell, actually the outer skeleton of the snail. But people still think of it as a "house" and envy the snail for being so lucky.

Another belief related to snails is that you can hear the roar of ocean waves when you hold the mouth of a snail shell against your ear. You do indeed hear a gentle murmur something like the breaking waves of distant surf. But you will hear the same sound if you put an empty cup or glass to your ear. A doctor might be able to tell you why you *seem* to hear the roar of the sea, for it has to do with the ear's inner structure.

Many people are offended by snails and slugs. They find them ugly and dislike their cold, clammy bodies and the unpleasant slime they leave behind. Charles Dickens, in his wonderful novel *David Copperfield*, wanted to give his readers a picture of the repulsive "umble" Uriah Heep. So he has David Copperfield find him "reading a great, fat book . . . his lank forefinger followed up every line as he read, and made clammy tracks along the pages (or so I thought) like a snail." In another novel, *Bleak House*, the same author said that the shiny, greasy rim of a hat resembled a "favorite snail-promenade." Many other authors have also created colorful descriptions through their references to snails.

More often than not, people who dislike snails dislike them because of the places they are found. Snails and slugs are night and rain creatures, and they often live in dank gloomy cellars and forest recesses, where the air is heavy and moist and full of the smell of mold and slow decay. In fact, they live together with such "unattractive" things as toads, black bugs, worms, spiders, fungus, and toadstools.

Snails without shells, the land slugs, are probably the most

This garden snail has left a shiny mucus track on the surface of the leaf.

widely and intensely hated of all land mollusks. Nobody, except possibly some slug expert, has anything nice to say about them. Even birds, squirrels, and other small forest mammals, which readily dine on snails, refuse to eat most slugs. Nevertheless, slugs are among the most successful of all land mollusks, being both numerous and widespread.

Not everyone, however, thinks of snails as dull. The famous eighteenth-century English poet, Robert Herrick, wrote a poem:

> Her pretty feet, like snails did creep
> A little out, and then,
> As if they played at bo-peep
> Did soon draw in again.

But he is unusual in this respect.

Children in many countries have rhymes about snails, which

they use in their games. Here are a few samples: "Snail, snail come out of your hole, Or else I'll beat you black as coal," and "Snail, snail, put out your horns, I'll give you bread and barley corns." These do not make much literal sense. But this one does: "Snail, snail, put out your horn, We want some rain to grow our corn." Snails do come out—and put out their "horns"—when the humidity rises before rain.

It is hard to believe that some species of lowly sea snails were once closely associated with the noblemen and emperors of ancient Rome. This species is the spiny murex snail that lives in large numbers in the Mediterranean Sea. In Roman times, the snails were gathered, their bodies and shells crushed, and eventually a lovely purple dye was extracted. Cloth stained with this dye was worn only by the senators, emperors, and noblemen of the Roman Empire. Most of this dye was made in the city of Tyre, now in Lebanon. For this reason, the color is often called Tyrian purple. It is also known as royal purple.

Although snails are not much use in medicine today, in nineteenth-century England, it was customary to mix the slime of snails in warm milk and give it to people to "strengthen" their lungs or as a cure for consumption. And in the Hebrew Talmud, the sentence appears: "God created the snail as a cure for the scab." Probably neither belief is correct.

Some Indian tribes of Colombia in South America believe that a certain kind of snail is able to keep away all sicknesses. They carry a specimen around with them because they think it can hide them from all the evil spirits that bring disease. Possibly they think this way because they see how well land snails can hide during a hot, dry spell. Thus they might reason that the same snails should be able to help them hide from evil, disease-bearing spirits.

Snails shells are used in many countries for religious purposes. The best known of these is the chank shell, a heavy, white species of sea snail found in the Indian and Pacific oceans.

17

It stands for the Hindu god Vishnu and is dedicated to him. Chank shells, like most gastropod shells, have the mouth of the shell on the right when they are held with the spire up. Sometimes a freak specimen appears in which the mouth is on the left. Such a chank shell is thought to be especially holy. Statues of the god Vishnu show him holding a left-handed, or sinistral, chank shell. Hindu doctors used to believe that medicine drunk from a chank shell would work better than medicine drunk from any other vessel.

Snail shells, cowrie shells in particular, have also been used as money by many cultures. Two species of cowrie were most commonly used this way. One comes from a small, yellowish snail living in vast numbers in many parts of the Indo-Pacific region. Its use as money was so widespread that it was named *Cypraea moneta* (money cowrie). The other species is about the same size and color, and has a narrow orange-colored ring on top.

These are a few of the unusual—and often incorrect—ideas people have had about snails and snail shells. There are many more. But, as we shall soon see, the real facts about snails and slugs are as remarkable as anything that has been thought of in myth, legend, or popular belief.

3
Marine Snails

About forty thousand different species of gastropods exist today. Most of them live in the oceans: of these marine gastropods, the greatest number reside in the shallow coral zones of tropical seas. Biologists believe that snails evolved many millions of years ago in the sea, and indeed, sea snails show the greatest variety of shapes and forms. Because snails first existed in the ocean, and because marine snails are among the most common animals of the seashore, they offer a good introduction to the body forms and life cycles of snails.

PARTS OF A SNAIL

At first inspection, the body of a snail may seem complicated and confusing. It may even be hard to tell just what or where something is. Their soft, flexible bodies always seem to be moving and changing shape, and they have the amazing ability to fold up, almost like accordions, when they wish to pull into their shells. But another reason for confusion has to do with a feature common to almost all snails. A major part of a snail's body is coiled. The coiled portion is usually on one side of the snail, giving the animal an unequal or one-sided (lopsided) appearance, and asymmetrical forms are more difficult to under-

19

stand than symmetrical forms. Nevertheless, all gastropods share a similar body plan which is modified in various ways in the different kinds of snails discussed in this book.

The structure of the body is most easily understood if you imagine you are looking down on the snail as it crawls over the ground. Imagine also that the shell is transparent, so that you can see inside it. It will appear that the snail's body is roughly divided into three parts. At the front of the snail is the first part, called the *head*. The head contains the mouth and one pair of fingerlike tentacles. At the base of each tentacle is an eye. The second part of the snail is the single, long, flattened *foot* on which the snail crawls. At the end of the foot, on top, is a hard disk. When the snail draws into its shell, the head is pulled in first, followed by the foot. As the foot disappears inside the

Diagram of top view of a snail.

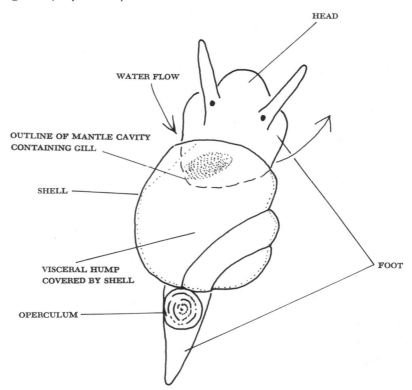

HEAD

WATER FLOW

OUTLINE OF MANTLE CAVITY
CONTAINING GILL

SHELL

VISCERAL HUMP
COVERED BY SHELL

FOOT

OPERCULUM

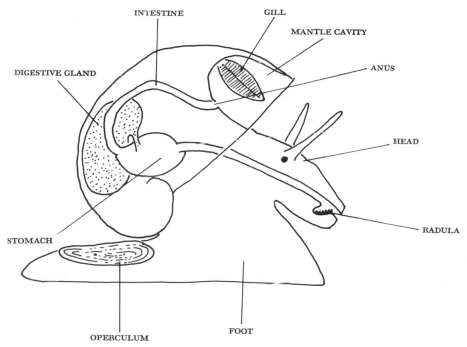

INTESTINE GILL MANTLE CAVITY ANUS DIGESTIVE GLAND HEAD RADULA STOMACH OPERCULUM FOOT

Diagram of side view of a snail.

shell, the disk clamps over the opening, like a lid topping a container; the disk protects the soft body of the snail from enemies who might otherwise force their way in. This hard disk is called an *operculum*, a Latin word meaning "lid" or "cover." In some snails, the operculum is made of hard shell-like calcium carbonate; in others, it is composed of a brown flexible material similar to the substance found in the horns and antlers of animals—and in our own fingernails.

The third distinct part of the snail's body is a large, coiled hump. Most of the important internal organs are found inside this hump: the stomach, digestive gland, heart, kidney, and the organs called *gonads*, which produce eggs or sperm. All these organs together are called the *viscera*, and so the snail's hump is called the *visceral hump*.

The Shell

The snail's shell is made by a special skin that covers the top of the snail's body like a sheet. It is firmly attached to the visceral hump, but hangs down around the body, including the head and foot, somewhat like a skirt. (Of course it doesn't cover the bottom surface of the foot.) This special skin is called a *mantle*, and it produces the shell material, calcium carbonate. The mantle and shell appear almost at the same time and develop together in the embryology of a snail. The mantle lines the inside of the shell and is responsible for thickening and strengthening it, and repairing any damage. Growth of the shell occurs only at the edge of the mantle lining the inside edge of the shell. Here the shell is often thin and sharp, because it is the newest portion of the shell. The oldest part of the shell is the pointed apex, or spire; it is often worn away and eroded.

A common garden snail with the top of the shell, the oldest part, showing erosion from age.

The calcium that snails need to construct their shells comes from seawater. Scientists have discovered that the new shell is actually produced within a very thin layer of seawater that is found between the shell and the edge of the mantle. Here, the chemicals from the sea and the mantle are brought together and formed into crystals of calcium carbonate that become the new shell. Biologists still have more to learn about how snails are able to construct their shells.

MANTLE CAVITY AND GILLS

Before taking a brief look at the gastropod's internal body, one important outer feature should be noted. There is a space between the skirt of the mantle and the head of a gastropod called the *mantle cavity*. Breathing, the discharge of waste materials from the snail's anus and kidney, as well as the passage of eggs and sperm all take place within the mantle cavity.

The mantle cavity contains the gill, which is the breathing organ of the snail. A gill is made up of hundreds of thin, skin-like flaps called *filaments*, arranged somewhat like the pages of a book. Each filament is covered with microscopic, hairlike cilia. The cilia move in a rhythmic beat and cause a flow of seawater into and out of the mantle cavity. As the seawater moves across the surface of the filaments, oxygen from the water passes into the filaments, and carbon dioxide—a waste material from the snail—passes out of the filaments into the seawater.

Most marine snails have only a single gill in their mantle cavities, although the most primitive marine snails have two gills. This group includes some of the seashore limpets and snails that have holes or slits, such as the keyhole limpets and the abalones. Because snails with two gills are thought to be direct descendents of the most ancient snails, scientists place them into the order called *Archeogastropoda*, meaning "ancient gastropods."

23

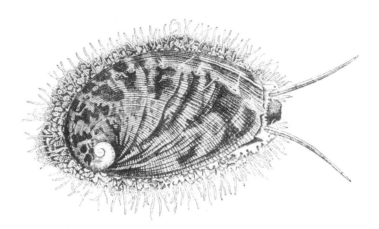

A drawing of a marine limpet-like abalone snail, an archeogastropod.

Since the waste products of the snail—coming from the anus and kidney—are discharged in the mantle cavity above the snail's head, it might seem that gastropods have a sewage disposal problem. However, the continuous flow of seawater into and out of the mantle cavity helps to move these materials away from the snail. Many snails have a long, tubelike siphon, an outgrowth of the mantle, which acts like an intake pipe. This arrangement ensures that the clean water flowing into the mantle is not contaminated by the snail's waste materials.

A dorsal view of a marine prosobranch snail. Note the siphon, tentacles, and extended foot. The dark area at the rear of the shell is the operculum.

All the marine snails that we have mentioned so far have operculums to close off the entrances to their shells, and one or two gills in their mantle cavities. Because the gills lie in front of the heart, which is located in the visceral hump, scientists put these snails into a subclass called the *Prosobranchia*, meaning "gills" (*branchia*) "in front" (*proso*). There is also another subclass of gastropods in which the gills lie *behind* the heart. The snails in this group bear the name *Opisthobranchia*, meaning "gills behind" (*opistho*). The opisthobranchs also differ from the prosobranchs because they hardly ever have an operculum. Indeed, many "hind-gillers" are in the process of losing their shells. All the beautiful sea slugs have lost their shells and are entirely naked. Many opisthobranchs still possess shells, although they are usually weak and too small to enclose the entire bodies of the snails. Such shells are called bubble shells because of their smooth, round, shiny appearance. Sometimes the shell of an opisthobranch is partly or entirely enclosed within the tissue of the mantle and no longer visible from the outside.

How a Snail Extends Its Foot to Move

If you have ever tried to pull the body of a snail out of its shell, you know that this is usually impossible. That's because a snail's body is attached to the inside of its shell by means of a large, powerful muscle. Branches of this muscle are attached to both the head and the foot. When a muscle contracts, it does work; for example, it may bend your arm, or in the case of a snail, pull the snail's foot into the shell. But when that muscle relaxes, no work is done. Your arm doesn't return to its original position unless other muscles contract to extend it again. With the snail, the work of extending the foot out of the shell must be accomplished by muscles acting in conjunction

An opisthobranch with a bubble shell. The fleshy portion of the snail visible here includes the head and foot. Snails like these spend time burrowing in sand.

with something else—water pressure! A snail's body has many interconnecting compartments that contain blood. Since its blood is similar to seawater, we can think of a snail's body as a sack containing seawater and other internal organs. The snail's foot in particular contains a large blood space. When muscles near the top of the foot contract, the blood is forced down to the bottom of the foot. Imagine a balloon filled with water. If you squeezed the top, the bottom would swell and extend. The foot of the snail is protruded from the shell in exactly the same way—by muscles at the junction of the foot and the head forcing blood into the spaces in the foot. When the snail contracts other muscles to retract back into the shell, the blood in the foot flows back up into a multitude of other small blood spaces found throughout much of the body. Unless the blood flowed back into the body at the same time that the muscles did their work, the foot would never fit into the shell. Imagine trying to pull an inflated balloon through a small hole. Even if the balloon were pulled by strong muscles, it wouldn't fit through the hole unless the air was permitted to escape. Likewise, the blood in the protruded foot of the snail must escape— into blood spaces in the body of the mollusk.

Once the foot is extended, how does the snail actually move? The flat, underneath portion of a snail's foot—the sole—contains many tiny muscles. In crawling, these muscles contract together, usually beginning at the back of the sole. The muscle contractions occur in waves, moving along the length of the foot. As these waves reach the forward edge of the foot, the sole is slightly lifted and stretched forward, then again touches down on the surface the snail is crawling along. Since the waves of contraction move continuously along the foot from back to front, the front edge is constantly being lifted and extended forward. In this way the entire sole gradually moves forward, giving the snail its gliding motion. Special glands in the foot produce a sticky mucus which continuously lubricates the foot during movement. Place a land snail on a glass plate and you will be able to observe the action of the foot through the glass. For snails living in water, the side of an aquarium will do quite well.

Some small snails move by cilia alone, without muscle contractions. The sole of the foot is covered with cilia, which beat in the same direction and slowly propel the snail along.

A snail's speed depends mostly on the size and shape of its shell. Species with large, bulky shells move very slowly, because they must drag their heavy shells behind them. But other gastropods have become more streamlined. Either the shell is less bulky, or the sides of the foot curl up and partially enclose the shell as the animal is crawling. This makes movement more efficient.

Snails move in two other ways. Some snails spend their lives drifting in the ocean. One type like this is the beautiful *Violet snail,* whose shells sometimes wash ashore along Florida beaches. Violet snails spend their lives feeding on jellyfish that drift in tropical ocean currents. The snails stay afloat by producing a bubble of air enclosed in a tough mucus-like substance secreted by a gland in the foot.

Some snails can swim, but as you might guess, swimmers are found in the subclass Opisthobranchia—snails that have either lost their shells, or that have very small thin shells. Some of these swimming opisthobranchs will be described later.

FEEDING AND DIGESTION

Marine snails eat a great variety of food. Snails that live on intertidal rocks, like the common periwinkles, are usually grazers, eating marine seaweeds or microscopic algae. Some species, such as the slipper limpets, use their gills to filter tiny drifting plant cells called *phytoplankton* (plant plankton) from the seawater. Most marine snails, however, are flesh-eaters. They eat either dead animals or live prey. Snails that feed on dead flesh are *scavengers*, while those that kill their own prey are *predators*.

No matter what kind of food a snail eats, all snails make use of a special kind of spiny, tonguelike structure called a *radula*. (In Latin the word *radulare* means "to scrape.") The radula consists of a long flat ribbon of horny material on which tiny jagged teeth are embedded and arranged in rows, like the teeth on a file. In use, the radula is partly extended from the snail's mouth and pulled back and forth by special muscles, much as a strip of sandpaper is pulled back and forth over the edge of a piece of wood. By this action, bits of food are rasped away and then carried into the mouth. As the rows of teeth that come into contact with the food get worn or broken away, new rows of teeth form and move forward to replace the old.

Rows of teeth on the radula of a freshwater snail. Each tooth contains a fringe of sharp hooks.

Find an aquarium with some snails in it and you will have a good way to observe a snail's radula in action. As a snail glides along the glass side of the aquarium, rasping the algae that grow there, the radula moving back and forth will be easy to see. In a marine aquarium, periwinkles show this nicely.

Although almost all marine snails have radulas, the shape of the teeth and the number of teeth in each row vary according to the kind of food the species eats. The shape and arrangement of teeth on the radula are therefore helpful in the classification of snails. The most primitive snails, archeogastropods, rasp plants: seaweeds and algae. Their radula is usually very wide, with large numbers of teeth, which seem well adapted for rasping food particles off of rocks and sweeping them into the mouth. Most snails have radulas that are narrower, with fewer teeth per row. Flesh-eaters often have sharp, piercing teeth; another group, which includes the poisonous cone snails, has only one long slender tooth shaped like a harpoon in each row.

Snails have a digestive tract that includes a stomach, intestine, and anus. Food particles are digested by special chemicals called *enzymes* that are produced within a special *digestive gland* connected to the stomach. This may sound similar to the structure in advanced animals, but there is a difference. In snails, food particles are moved along the digestive tract by cilia rather than by muscles, as is the case with most higher animals. As you might guess, this means that the process of moving masses of food along the digestive tract is much slower in snails. Also, food particles are stuck together by *mucus*, a slimy material produced throughout the digestive tract. The cilia move the strings of sticky food along.

REPRODUCTION

All living organisms must give rise to offspring like themselves, and marine snails have a variety of interesting ways for making certain that enough young are produced to ensure that each generation of snails will survive to mature and reproduce. In the largest subclass of gastropods, the prosobranchs (front-gillers), a snail is either male or female. The most primitive prosobranchs, members of the order Archeogastropoda, shed eggs and sperm by the millions directly into the sea. Although enormous quantities of eggs and sperm are wasted by this haphazard method, some eggs do manage to come into contact with sperm and become fertilized. The fertilized eggs quickly develop into microscopic, top-shaped, ciliated creatures called *trochophores*. A trochophore, in spite of its tiny size, has a complete digestive tract and is able to feed on the phytoplankton cells drifting in the sea. Since the trochophore can be carried by ocean currents, biologists call this stage a *larva*. Soon, the trochophore larva begins to form a tiny shell. Small veil-like folds appear on the part of the larva that will become the head, and these develop into a structure called the *velum*. At this stage, the larva is called a *veliger* ("veil-bearer"). The velum is very important to the larva. The beating cilia on the velum propel the larva through the water and also create tiny water currents that direct food particles toward the mouth of the veliger. The larval shell continues to grow and begins to change from a cap-shaped shell to a coiled shell. Soon a foot and tiny operculum appear. Except for its ciliated velum, a veliger larva at this stage resembles a tiny, free-swimming snail. After a period of time, days or weeks depending on the species, the veliger settles to the bottom and takes up life as a baby snail. The velum becomes part of the tiny snail's head, and as the snail grows, the velum disappears. In the meantime, ocean currents may have carried the veliger many miles or even hundreds of miles from the place where its parents lived. Thus, through the drifting of the veliger larva, marine snail species disperse great distances, establishing populations in new places.

In the more specialized prosobranchs (front-gillers), the eggs and sperm are not released directly into the sea. Rather, the male snails have evolved a special organ for transferring sperm directly to the female. This organ is called the *penis*, and it is located on the right side of the snail just behind the head.

After the eggs are fertilized— inside the body of the female— a special gland in the female's body produces a tough capsule around all the eggs. But before this happens, each fertilized egg is provided with a supply of yolk. Yolk is a nutritious substance that supplies energy for the developing embryo. The

31

female gastropod has special glands within her body that produce the yolk. The female then deposits the egg capsules on shells, rocks, pilings, seaweeds, and many other objects, and usually the capsules are firmly attached. Generally, a single egg capsule will contain many developing embryos, but in some species, an egg capsule contains only one. And in some, the capsules are not attached at all, but released to drift in the ocean currents.

While most marine prosobranchs abandon their egg masses after attaching them to a convenient object, some species stay with their eggs and protect them during development. This is called *brooding*. Brooding is not very common in marine snails, probably because brooding mothers are unable to carry out other important functions of life while remaining in one place with the egg capsules.

Inside the egg capsules, each fertilized egg begins to divide, producing more and more cells. In this way, each fertilized egg cell becomes an embryo. In some species, the embryo becomes a veliger larva that emerges from the egg capsule and swims away. In many other species, the veligers remain inside the capsule and continue to develop until they look like tiny models of their parents. Then they crawl out of the capsule and take up their own lives as juvenile snails. There are even some marine snails that produce live young. These species don't form egg capsules because the embryos develop inside their mother's body.

Predator Snails

Snails have absolutely fascinating feeding habits, far more remarkable than one might imagine from their small size and slow pace. The first snails to evolve millions of years ago in the primeval seas probably ate seaweeds or marine plants of some kind, or perhaps decaying plant material. Even today, the most primitive living archeogastropods feed on these materials.

Baby marine prosobranch snails developing inside their capsules, almost ready to hatch. Notice the black eye-spots on some of the babies.

But as life developed and other kinds of animals became more abundant in the ancient seas, many gastropods changed their feeding habits. Today, food for the majority of marine snails comes not from plants but from animals. Many snails have evolved the ability to kill and consume animal prey. Some species, such as the larger whelks, overcome their prey by what can only be described as sheer brute strength. The mollusks most often eaten by whelks are bivalves such as clams, oysters, and mussels. The only defense they have is to close their shells tightly. Of course, this doesn't work against whelks. Attacking a clam or an oyster, the whelk forces the edge of its strong shell between the two valves and pushes its snout through the narrow gap. Soon the clam is killed and eaten. Other conchs hold their prey using their foot and, with the edge of their shell, chip away at the prey's shell until its soft body is exposed. Smaller whelks, such as the common crown conch of Florida, rely less on brute strength and more on patience. The crown conch waits until the prey ventures out of its shell in search of food or fresh seawater. Then the crown conch pounces, and in a short time the flesh is devoured.

This marine whelk is a fierce predator. Notice the siphonal canal of the shell and the siphon extending forward.

Most predatory snails have a special tubelike extension from their head called a *proboscis*. The proboscis is operated by several small muscles inside the snail's head and can be pulled back into the head when not in use. The proboscis is really a flexible extension of the snail's head; it contains the mouth and radula. With their proboscises, some snails can probe into small marine animals such as barnacles in order to rasp and suck their bodies. In other cases, the proboscis can be extended deep into holes or crevices to search for hidden prey.

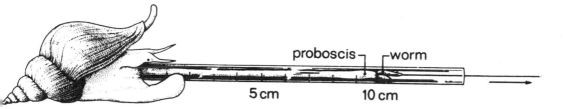

A *drawing of a marine whelk attempting to eat a worm that has been placed inside a tube, to see how far the whelk's proboscis will extend. It reaches ten centimeters, about four inches.*

Many snails have combined the use of the proboscis with another valuable skill—the ability to actually bore holes through the shells of their prey. Perhaps you have seen clam or oyster shells on the beach, each with a perfectly neat, circular hole in it. Before drilling a hole, the snail first secretes some chemicals to soften the shell. Then the radula rasps out the softened shell. This process is repeated until the hole is complete; it may take several hours to a day or more, depending on the thickness of the shell. During this time, the victim is either held in place by the foot of the snail, or the snail may just remain attached to the site of the hole while the prey moves about. When the hole is completed, the proboscis is inserted through the bored hole and the clam's body is soon eaten. Snails devour not only clams, oysters, and mussels in this manner, but also a variety of other marine animals like barnacles and moss animals (bryozoa). Snails are able to fast for relatively long periods without harm. After feeding, it may be several days before another mussel or oyster is attacked.

The "rock snails" of the large family Muricidae, which includes the oyster drills that cause so much damage to oysters along the East Coast of the United States, attack prey living on the sea bottom. Other borer snails crawl underneath the sand or mud and attack their prey from below. Moon snails behave this way. A biologist in New England has shown that a large moon snail can probably consume the better part of a bushel of delicious soft-shelled or steamer clams during a single season.

A mass of oyster drills attached, for a free ride, to the back of a horseshoe crab. (The snails do not harm the crab.)

Cone snails, which prey on fairly large, active animals such as sea worms, other gastropods, or even small fish, display one of the most interesting methods of feeding. The tooth in the radula of a cone snail is hollow, barbed, and shaped like a tiny harpoon. A special poison gland in the snail's head provides the tooth with poison. When the cone snail attacks, the proboscis, containing the harpoon tooth, strikes the prey, almost the way a snake strikes. The harpoon tooth is shot into the prey and the poison is injected through it. When the prey stops struggling, which doesn't take long because of the poison, it is swallowed whole. The proboscis may strike repeatedly, but each strike requires a new tooth, since the harpoon remains inside the body of the prey. After each strike, the next tooth on the radula moves into position, ready for attack.

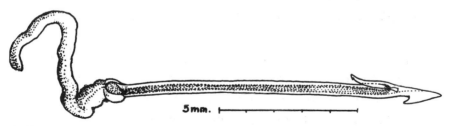

A drawing of a radula tooth of a cone snail, showing its harpoon-like shape.

The poison of some of the larger cone snails living in the Pacific Ocean is known to be dangerous to humans. To be safe, never handle a living cone snail, and never pick up a cone shell unless you are certain that the live animal is not inside. Cone snails are found only in tropical oceans.

SNAILS THAT CHANGE SEX

A marine snail commonly found along both the Atlantic and Pacific shores is the slipper limpet. Slipper limpets have low, cuplike shells, with a shelf of shell extending outward from one end, giving the shell a shape that resembles a lady's slipper.

Slipper limpets are unusual in that all individuals change sex during their lifetimes. Baby limpets begin life as males, but eventually switch to females as they grow older. Slipper limpets are usually found in groups of at least two individuals, a smaller (younger) male perched near the edge of a larger female. Thus, the male can extend its penis around the edge of the female's shell in order to fertilize the eggs inside the body of the female. Some slipper limpets are stacked, one on top of another, to form chains of individuals. The largest snails at the bottom are always female, and the smaller animals at the top of the stack are males. The intermediate animals along the chain are frequently at some stage in between. As the larger, older females die, younger females take their place, and then some of the males change sex. Thus, the chain of individuals is something like a family, with males always present to fertilize the females.

This pattern of sexual reproduction is ideal for slipper limpets because these snails are unable to actively crawl about. They tend to remain in one place where their gills filter large quantities of seawater, bringing them microscopic phytoplankton. Since the snails do not move very much, they would have a difficult time finding partners for mating. Fortunately, the adults do not have to search for them. Instead, the veliger larvae search for adult snails on which to settle. The veliger larvae quickly develop into tiny juvenile slipper limpets resembling their parents. But unlike the adults, the baby slipper limpets are active crawlers. Thus, even if some veligers don't find an adult on which to settle, the juveniles that develop from the veligers can search actively for a permanent perch.

Marine snails that belong to the subclass Opisthobranchia (hind-gillers) reproduce much the same way as the prosobranchs, but there is one big difference. Whereas the prosobranchs are either male or female, the opisthobranchs have both sexes united in a single individual. They are hermaphrodites, a word derived from the names of two Greek gods; Hermes, the male god, and Aphrodite, the female god. When we consider the opisthobranchs—and also the land snails, which are thought to be descended from opisthobranchs—it will be clear that this method of sexual reproduction has some very useful benefits.

All the snails discussed in this chapter live in the sea. But some of their ancestors were not content to stay there. They first invaded brackish water in estuaries (places where seawater mixes with fresh water), and then freshwater areas. Finally, some moved to the land. Let us look into these groups now.

4

Freshwater Snails

Snails are familiar animals in fresh water, occurring commonly in ponds, lakes, streams, rivers, and even in temporary pools that may dry up for long periods at a time. Some freshwater snails are similar in appearance to marine prosobranch snails. They have typical gills in their mantle cavities with which they breathe, and they are able to close off the entrances to their shells with operculums. These freshwater prosobranchs are in fact closely related to marine snails. Some are quite large, with shells often reaching eight to ten centimeters (three to four inches); many others are quite small, often less than five millimeters.

Most freshwater prosobranchs are rather drab in appearance, with grayish bodies and brown or tan shells that are usually smooth. While some species burrow into bottom sediments, most crawl along the underside of rocks. Thus freshwater prosobranch snails often have powerful feet, which allow them to cling tightly in rushing streams and rapids.

Some of the best places to see freshwater prosobranchs are the mountain regions of South Carolina, Georgia, Alabama, and Tennessee. Here many species occur in scores of different shapes with a great variety of shell ornamentation. Biologists place these snails in the family named *Pleuroceridae*, a word meaning "ribbed horn-snail." This refers to the shape of the shell and to the ridges that form the ornamentation.

Because some pleurocerid snails live only in very restricted river systems, and because water pollution and dam construction affects the lives of these animals, certain species are in danger of extinction. One such snail is called *Io*, named after a Greek river nymph. *Io* lives only in rapids of mountain streams in the Tennessee River system. *Io* evolved here and never spread to other river systems. It spends its whole life clinging to rocks by means of its suction-cup-like foot, even in the most rapidly flowing water. Unfortunately, the rivers in which *Io* flourishes have been dammed up by the Tennessee Valley Authority to provide flood relief and water power for the people in the southeastern United States. Formerly rushing rivers have been turned into sluggish streams or huge lakes—places where *Io* is unable to live because they are not as rich in oxygen. This attractive American snail is in danger of vanishing forever.

Another family of freshwater prosobranchs contains the snails commonly called *mystery snails*. Mystery snails do not lay eggs. Instead, the young develop inside the bodies of the females and are born as tiny juveniles. Perhaps this accounts for the name "mystery snail." You may put such a snail into your aquarium one day and the next day find the tank filled with many baby snails.

Because mystery snails give birth to live young, zoologists place them in a family called *Viviparidae*, from *vivi* ("live") and *pari* ("birth"). One advantage of giving birth to live young is that the babies end up in the same general area as the parent snails—an area that is clearly a suitable place to live. Because the babies cannot crawl very far away, large numbers of such snails will be found in favorable places.

Viviparid snails are found in bodies of fresh water in many parts of the world. Most of them have brown or green shells, large, plain, and smooth. But there are some that have sculptured shells with strong, revolving ridges of small regular beads; these shells look like decorated brooches. The most attractive species lives only in the Coosa River in Alabama and is called *Tulotoma magnifica,* a fitting name for this magnificent viviparid mystery snail. Unfortunately, their numbers have been greatly reduced by pollution and the accumulation of soft mud and silt. Since viviparid snails have no way to remove mud or silt from their gills, they must live only in clear waters. It seems that the future is grim for *Tulotoma,* too. Many collectors fear that this species may have already vanished.

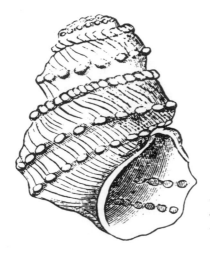

A drawing of Tulotoma magnifica, *a species of freshwater prosobranch very rare or perhaps extinct.*

Another interesting freshwater snail is the apple snail, which produces a round shell almost as large as an apple and lives in bodies of fresh water in the warmer countries of the world. The strange thing about this snail is that it can breathe in either air or water. When the water is foul and oxygen is in short supply, the snail can make part of its foot into a tube that extends out of the water like a snorkel. The apple snail can thus breathe fresh air through its snorkel. In clean water with plenty of dissolved oxygen, apple snails use their gills for breathing, like other front-gillers. It is therefore possible for these snails

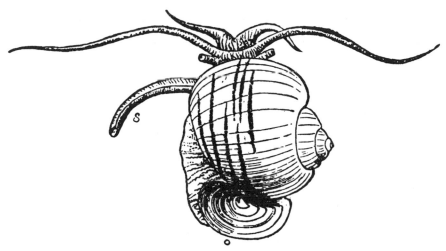

A drawing of an apple snail, showing the long snorkel-like siphon (letter S) and the operculum (letter O).

to live in canals and swamps, where the water is often stagnant, as well as in bodies of clean water.

Apple snails leave the water to lay their eggs on the upper parts of sedge grasses, the sides of boats, wharf pilings, driftwood, and other places. The eggs, produced by the hundreds, are small and have a rather hard, white shell. When the water level rises, as may happen after a storm, and the eggs are submerged in water for a few hours, they hatch and little snails crawl out to begin their own lives.

THE SNAILS OF LAKE TANGANYIKA

Lake Tanganyika lies in eastern Africa between Tanzania and Zambia. It is large and deep and contains some very unusual freshwater gastropods. European explorers in Africa in the nineteenth century noticed that many of the snails living there looked like marine snails. They had coarse, heavy shells and in many other ways made people think of ocean snails. And yet, the water of Lake Tanganyika is quite fresh. How did this come about?

The first guess was that in ancient times Lake Tanganyika had been connected to the ocean and that ocean snails had lived there. After the connection was broken, the waters of the lake slowly turned fresh as rainwater washed into the lake over thousands of years. The snails kept their marine shape but adapted to life in fresh water.

This guess was soon abandoned when it was learned that there never was a connection between the lake and the ocean. In some ways, however, this large lake is much like the ocean. Lake Tanganyika has high cliffs, deep water, rocky beaches, and huge waves caused by violent storms. Under these ocean-like conditions, it is thought, the freshwater snails evolved into oceanlike forms. This is called *convergent evolution*: distantly related animal species "converge" into similar forms because they live under similar conditions. Convergent evolution is common in nature and has often led scientists to false conclusions, as in the case of the snails of Lake Tanganyika.

Freshwater Lung Breathers

Prosobranchs are not the only snails that live in fresh water. There is another, entirely different group of freshwater snails. These are easily recognized because, unlike the freshwater prosobranchs, they do not possess operculums. Like the proso-branchs, they live in fresh water, lay their eggs, and find their food there. But unlike most prosobranchs, at least every few hours they must come to the surface to breathe.

This kind of snail has lost its gill but has evolved a type of lung inside its mantle cavity. Zoologists place the air-breathing snails into a subclass separate from the snails with gills. In Latin the word for lung is *pulmo* (from which we get our word pulmonary, meaning "lung"). For this reason, the name *Pulmonata* (pulmonates) was given to the air-breathing gastro-pods. Thus we find that two subclasses of snails live in fresh water: gill-bearing prosobranchs and lung-bearing pulmonates.

44

Pulmonate snails are actually much more common on land; relatively few kinds live in fresh water, and even fewer in the sea. In fact, zoologists believe that the freshwater pulmonates evolved from ancestors that originally lived on land.

There are several kinds of freshwater pulmonates that are easy to recognize. All have thin, fragile shells, usually some shade of brown or tan in color. The *pond snails* have a high spire, and some species grow quite large, up to thirty-five millimeters (about one and one-half inches), while others are small, only up to twelve millimeters (one-half inch). The scientific name for the pond snails is *Lymnaea,* from the Greek word meaning a "pond" or "marsh," and there are many species in this group.

The *tadpole snails* have a shell with a large last coil (called the *body whorl*) and a low spire. Tadpole snails are easy to recognize because, when the shell is placed so that the pointed spire is up, the opening, or mouth, of the shell is on the left. Pond snails, on the other hand, have the opening on the right, as do most snails. Tadpole snails are called *Physa,* from the Greek word for "bellows."

The *wheel* or *ramshorn snails* have flat, circular shells with-

Side view of freshwater tadpole snail. Note the contrast between the large body whorl and the low spire. The mantle cavity is easy to see.

out raised spires. These shells do indeed resemble wheels or rams' horns. Another group of freshwater pulmonates are *limpets*. Freshwater limpets are usually hard to see and quite small. They are only five millimeters in length and can be found in streams on the underside of rocks, on dead freshwater clam shells, bits of submerged wood, and the leaves of pond plants. Their name is *Ancylus*, from the Greek word that means "hooked" or "curved."

Pulmonates are common in nature, and some species grow well in an aquarium. People who breed freshwater tropical fish frequently keep some of these pulmonates in their tanks to eat the algae which grows on the glass sides of the aquarium. Very often, the snails are much easier to grow than the fish!

When freshwater ponds and streams become polluted, all freshwater mollusks suffer, but the pulmonates have an advantage over the prosobranchs. Since prosobranchs must extract their oxygen from water, they quickly die when water pollution becomes so bad that oxygen disappears from the water. The pulmonates, however, can rely on air for the oxygen they need. For this reason, it is not uncommon to see large populations of robust tadpole snails living in polluted water where no other snails are found.

BREATHING IN WATER

Biologists have been interested in discovering how pulmonates, which evolved from land snails and possess lungs for breathing, have become adapted to living in fresh water. Some species live only in very wet places, such as marshes, swamps, and wet meadows, and are not truly adapted to living in water. While they may occasionally be covered with water, they need not be considered freshwater snails because they must come to the land to breathe. Other pulmonates, however, have developed the ability to breathe while submerged. In these species, the mantle cavity fills up with water, and enough oxygen passes into the body from the water that the snails are able to live. Still other pulmonates come to the surface for a bubble of air, which they then carry in their mantle cavities as they crawl along the bottom of lakes or ponds. There are two advantages to this. First, they carry a supply of oxygen with them, as do scuba divers with their tanks of air, and so they do not need to return to the surface so often to replenish their supply. Another advantage to the air bubble is that it makes the snail more buoyant in water; the snail finds it easier to move around and uses less energy than it would without the bubble.

Other freshwater pulmonates have a still more amazing adaptation for breathing underwater. It came to light when scientists discovered that the air bubbles in the mantle cavities of some species contained mostly nitrogen gas. It has been shown that these snails use their bubbles in a much different way than divers use their air tanks. Because of the high concentration of nitrogen, the bubble acts something like a gill. Oxygen passes into the bubble from the surrounding water and is then taken up by the snail's tissue. Waste carbon dioxide, which all animals produce, enters the bubble from the snail's body and then passes from the bubble into the surrounding water. Thus, the nitrogen bubble does the job that a gill would do, if the snail had a gill. Snails with this type of bubble never have to return to the surface to breathe. This helps explain how some freshwater pulmonates can live in very deep water. They don't have to make long trips to the surface to take a breath.

The tiny freshwater limpets have solved the problem of breathing in quite a different way. They have given up the lung and evolved a new type of gill, different from the original prosobranch gill. Thus, these little snails could be considered the pulmonates best adapted for life in fresh water.

In the nineteenth century, sheep farmers in England found that their flocks were being attacked by a fatal disease called *liver rot*, in which the livers were destroyed and the sheep died. Soon people noticed that only sheep browsing in wet meadows near ponds and rivers suffered from the disease. Sheep in dry meadows seemed to be immune. This was one clue.

A search of the wet meadows showed that the ground was damp enough to enable many small freshwater snails to migrate from ponds and rivers to the moist grasses that the sheep ate. As the sheep swallowed the grasses, they also swallowed some snails. Here was another clue.

Scientists soon discovered that the snails were the innocent carriers of a small but deadly parasite called the *liver fluke*. Flukes are tiny wormlike animals closely related to the common flatworms (called planarians) found in ponds and streams. When a fluke-bearing snail was swallowed by a sheep, the fluke was not digested with the rest of the snail's body. Instead, the fluke made its way to the sheep's liver. There it stayed, slowly consuming the liver tissue, and eventually causing the death of its host. When scientists discovered the connection between snails in the meadow and flukes in the livers of sheep, prevention of liver rot was easy: fence off the wet meadows and keep the sheep out.

Freshwater snails are also the carriers of blood flukes, parasites which cause a serious disease that attacks large numbers of people in many parts of the world. Doctors call this disease *schistosomiasis* after the Latin name for the blood fluke, *Schistosoma*; but the disease is also called snail fever. People get this disease as part of a complicated chain of events in the life cycle of the blood fluke.

The eggs of the adult blood flukes are found in ponds, drainage ditches, rice paddies, and streams. The eggs are introduced

A handful of freshwater snails that transmit the blood fluke responsible for schistosomiasis.

into these places mixed with human waste matter, mainly feces and urine, which in many parts of the world are deposited directly into streams and lakes or are used as fertilizers in fields and rice paddies. In the water, each blood fluke egg hatches, releasing a microscopic creature that seeks out and burrows into the body of a certain species of freshwater snail. Once inside the snail's body, the microscopic parasite grows, multiplies, and assumes a different shape. Eventually, a multitude of very small wormlike creatures—all the descendents of the original animal that burrowed into the snail—burrow out of the snail's body into the surrounding water. Each of these creatures is called a *cercaria* (from the Greek word *kerkos*, meaning "tail"). A cercaria is barely visible to the unaided eye. It is extremely active and has a forked tail, which it uses to swim. Now each cercaria looks for a human being. Anybody wading in the water at such a time, even for a few minutes, can be attacked by the tiny cercaria. Using special chemicals (called enzymes), the cercaria produces a tiny hole in the skin and makes its way into a small blood vessel. This process is rapid and, like a mosquito bite, painless. The cercaria is carried through the body by the blood stream. Eventually it lodges in certain blood vessels and develops directly into an adult blood fluke. Here it feeds on blood and produces eggs, which eventually pass out of the body in waste matter. Blood flukes weaken the host, making it difficult for the sufferer to work. Usually

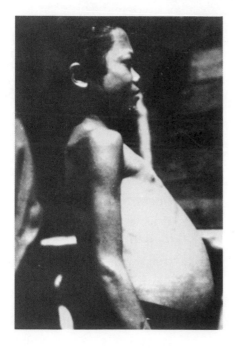

An advanced case of schistosomiasis.

a victim's arms become thin, the muscles flabby, and the stomach hard and bloated. Because of weakness, people suffering from this disease easily fall prey to other diseases. Millions of people in Africa, India, China, Japan, Southeast Asia, the West Indies, and elsewhere in warmer countries are victims of this disease.

Relatively few kinds of freshwater snails carry blood flukes. However, freshwater snails are the hosts of many parasitic diseases of domestic and wild animals, like the case of the snails bearing liver flukes discussed above. For this reason, freshwater snails have been studied much more extensively than many other kinds of gastropods.

SALT-MARSH SNAILS

Not all aquatic pulmonates live in ponds and other bodies of fresh water. Some are found abundantly in saltwater marshes in many parts of the world, where they live on grasses or under pieces of wood. Some very large species of marsh pulmonates live in Africa and Asia, with shells reaching eighty millimeters (about three inches) in height. In the Northern Hemisphere, marsh pulmonates are smaller. Looking rather like tadpole snails except for their shells opening on the right, marsh snails are common in salt marshes and are especially conspicuous at high tide. At that time, they climb to the tops of the salt-marsh grasses to avoid being covered by water. Because many of these snails have black feet, their scientific names is *Melampus* (meaning "black foot" in Greek). Melampus snails eat decomposing plant matter and detritus and are themselves eaten by marsh birds and small rodents such as field mice.

5
Snails on Land

Some people are surprised to learn that snails and snail shells are found on land. They think that all snails live in water, but this is not so.

A large group of snails is able to live on land. They breathe air, eat food found on land, breed and lay their eggs on land; in short, they spend their entire lives on land. And, strange as it may seem, these snails live all around us. We have only to know where to look for them. Some live on the ground in parks and forests, under leaves, under the bark of fallen tree trunks, or under loose rocks. Others live high on trees and crawl to the ground only to lay their eggs. Some land snails are even found in hot deserts, and still others are found high in the mountains. In fact, land snails often turn up in the most unlikely places: in window flowerpots in the heart of big cities, among the stones in the roadbed of railroads, even crawling up the sides of garage walls in the suburbs. They love dank cellars and the underside of stone benches and stone fences. It is difficult to turn over wet rubbish in neglected city lots and not find a few snails. Often the snails are very small, only a few millimeters in size, but snails they are, and all around us. Let us look a little more closely at these shy but highly successful land dwellers.

Land snails nestling in a palm leaf.

Two Kinds of Land Snails

First of all, not counting the land slugs (discussed later), there are two different kinds of land snails. One group is far larger than the other and probably more familiar. The snails in this group have no lids or operculums to close up their shells. Each of them breathes through a breathing pore located behind the head. This pore leads into the mantle cavity and to the lung. If you look closely at one of these snails, you can see its pore opening and closing as it breathes. These snails are first cousins to the air-breathing freshwater snails discussed in the previous chapter, but since they live on land, they are called land, or terrestrial, pulmonates.

Every land pulmonate has two long "horns" (actually, tentacles) on the top of its head and two smaller tentacles below. Its eyes are located at the tips of the longer tentacles and look like two black, shiny dots. The tentacles with the eyes can be pulled into the snail's head, in the way that the fingers of a glove can be pulled back from the inside.

The other group of land snails is less familiar to most people. The members of this group are like terrestrial pulmonates in most respects, but they differ by having operculums and by having only two tentacles instead of four. Also, their eyes lie at the base of the tentacles. But like pulmonates, they have lost their gills and breathe air using a lung. These snails are very close relatives of the marine and freshwater prosobranchs; in fact, they are land prosobranchs.

A land prosobranch. Notice the operculum (arrow) *and the eyes at the base of the tentacles.*

The land prosobranchs are common in the mountains of Cuba, Jamaica, Puerto Rico, Hispaniola, and elsewhere in the West Indies. Large populations are also present in China, India, Southeast Asia, Africa, and South and Central America. A single species is found in much of Central and Western Europe. There are only seven species in the United States, five in Florida, and one each in Texas and the Midwest.

SNAIL BREATHING

All life began in the sea. When some of the animals left the sea to live on land, they had to overcome the great difficulties of a new environment, difficulties that were not present in the sea. One of the most important tasks was how to keep from losing body water and drying out. Biologists say that all land creatures are like wandering water tanks: water must be kept inside the body, and water lost from the body must be quickly replaced.

How do land snails keep the water in their bodies from evaporating? The land prosobranchs have a simple solution. When the weather is too dry, they find a hiding place, withdraw into their shells, pull up their operculums, and stay that way until the rains come. In the West Indies, where land prosobranchs are common, one can pass a stone wall without seeing a single live snail. But if one returns after even a light shower, snails are there, as thick as flies on a garbage heap. But when the weather is dry again, a snail collector has to turn over rocks and grub in the dead leaves in order to come up with even a few. If the dry weather lasts a very long time, many prosobranchs perish; their dried-up bodies remain inside their shells until the operculums drop off. That is why one can always find numerous empty snail shells on the ground in places where prosobranchs are common. The snails that find wetter hiding places, however, do survive to carry on the species.

How do land pulmonates preserve their body moisture? One

would think that they would have a harder time of it, without operculums to keep in the moisture. But the pulmonates have their own tricks. Each land pulmonate has a fleshy collar around the edge of its mantle cavity in such a way that the mantle cavity is closed except for a breathing pore. This breathing pore is most important to the snail. It opens to let air in and closes while the body takes up oxygen and releases carbon dioxide. Then it opens again to let the oxygen out and more fresh air in. Only a small amount of water vapor is allowed to escape through the breathing pore. The driest air in the world is found in deserts; rain can be lacking for years at a time. Nevertheless, there are snails that have adapted to desert life. In the desert regions in Arizona, New Mexico, and California, snails have to hide deep down under the rocks until rain falls. In the deserts of the Mideast, the snails lie in the open and look like lots of small round white stones. Their protection from the heat comes from their thick, heavy shells; in addition, their white color reflects the sun's rays, thus keeping the inside of the shell cooler. How well these snails have adapted to dryness can be seen in the case of a snail from the Egyptian desert (called *Erminia desertorum* for that reason) that was stored, simply pasted to a card, in the shell collection of the British Museum. After four years in the display case, it suddenly came to life and tried to crawl away. There is also the example of a desert snail from Mexico that revived after having spent six years asleep in a dark, dry museum drawer.

These snails were pulmonates. But the prosobranchs are not so lucky. Their mantle cavities remain wide open to the air, so air flows freely in and out. There is no breathing pore to control moisture and prevent its escape. This is not a problem as long as the air is very moist (about ninety-five percent humidity) or they find a place to hide. But when it becomes even a little drier, the land prosobranchs begin to lose body moisture rapidly, much more rapidly than the pulmonates. Then these snails have to hide, close up quickly, and rest until the next rains come. They can conserve only a little body moisture, enough to keep them alive but not enough to allow them to move around. Thus, pulmonates can breed more often and produce more young than prosobranchs. Consequently, land pulmonates are more successful, especially in places where both wet and dry seasons exist.

During periods of dry weather, land prosobranchs may have to wait a long time before they can come out of their shells. And during this time, they require oxygen. But how can they get oxygen into their lungs if their operculums are tightly sealed? They have solved this problem in a fascinating way. The shells of some land prosobranchs have tiny tubes that are in direct contact with air, even when the operculums are in place. Thus the land prosobranchs are able to continue breathing through a sort of land snorkel. The tubes are small—just large enough to allow air in without losing very much moisture.

SEX IN LAND SNAILS

Like all animals, land snails must reproduce, and they are really quite good at it! As you will soon see, this is another reason why there are so many more pulmonate land snails in the world than prosobranchs. Earlier we noted that marine prosobranchs had separate sexes: each individual was either male or female. This is also true of the land prosobranchs. Thus in every population of land prosobranchs, only the females can lay eggs. Moreover, in order to mate, males must search and find females.

With the pulmonates, on the other hand, every individual is both male and female at the same time. Every snail in any pulmonate population is able to lay eggs. The pulmonate snails do not have an arduous search for partners because they are able to mate with any other pulmonate snails they meet, provided they are the same species. No wonder pulmonates breed

Courting land snails showing one snail probing its mate (arrow).

so rapidly and no wonder it's so hard to get rid of the pesky ones in fields and gardens.

Does this mean that eventually all land prosobranchs will die out and that only pulmonates will remain? Probably not. As long as rain forests with heavy, reliable rainfall exist, there will probably always be terrestrial prosobranchs as well as pulmonates. In such areas, prosobranchs can make a successful stand against their rivals.

All land snails, prosobranchs as well as pulmonates, hatch directly from eggs. When the baby snail hatches, looking much like a miniature of its parents, all it has to do is eat and grow. It does not have to change its shape, as the veligers of many marine snails must.

Eggs are laid mostly in holes dug in the ground; some snails lay their eggs under rocks or bits of wood or leaves. Land snails produce far smaller numbers of eggs than marine snails. Often a clutch consists of only thirty to forty small round white or glassy eggs.

The mating habits of some land pulmonates are strange. One of the most unusual is found in the large family of *Helix* land snails. (*Helix* means "coil" in Greek; the *Helix* snails, like all snails, have coiled or spiral shells.) When two *Helix* snails interested in mating come together, they circle each other, sometimes for a long while. Finally they bring their bodies together and then each snail suddenly jabs a small, hard, pointed dart into the body of its partner. The dart comes from a special sac in which it is formed, and each *Helix* species has its own specially shaped dart. Now the snails exchange packets of sperm to fertilize each other's eggs. Later, each snail lays a batch of eggs and eventually many young are hatched.

There seems to be good reason for this strange behavior. Snails cannot see very well and thus they cannot, by sight alone, be sure that their partners are snails of the same species. The dancelike circling movement and the shape of the darts seem to be signs by which snails are able to recognize their proper mates. It is also possible that the piercing darts act as exciters. But no one really knows.

Helix land snail.

Food of Land Snails

Most land snails are vegetarians. They eat plants and vegetables, either fresh or slightly overripe, as well as decomposing plant matter. But there are also predatory snails that dine on earthworms and even other snails. Unfortunately, many of the plant-eaters seem to prefer the same foods we eat, and gardeners consider these snails pests. Still other snails prefer to eat fungus, which grows in the rotting leaves, and these are not pests. On the contrary, by chewing up dead leaves to get to the fungus, they help decompose the litter on the forest floor. Other fungus-eaters are even more directly useful. These snails eat the fungi that attacks and harms trees. In Jamaica, the owners of orange plantations collect such snails from trees in the forest and deliberately place them on their trees in order to prevent attacks by fungi.

But other plant-eating land snails can be a real menace. Probably the most destructive one is the giant African snail called *Achatina*, meaning "agate" snail. The shells of *Achatina* are

Giant African land snail (Achatina), *the largest ever photographed. Fountain pen is for comparison.*

In certain parts of Africa, the giant African land snail is gathered and sold for food in the markets.

large, about fifteen centimeters (six inches) in height, about the size of a large pear. The animal is even larger—its fleshy body stretches out to about eighteen centimeters (more than seven inches).

These snails were spread beyond their original home in Africa primarily by having been accidentally transported on fruit cargo ships. During the Second World War, the Japanese also shipped large numbers of these snails to Pacific islands they had conquered to provide food for their soldiers. When the Japanese were forced out, nobody wanted to eat the snails. Now *Achatina* snails are found in much of the Pacific region and have even appeared in Hawaii, California, and Florida.

Achatina eats many kinds of tropical fruits and vegetables and causes huge losses to farmers. The snails once destroyed the entire tea crop on the island of Sri Lanka (Ceylon). They are offensive in other ways, too. Because of their large size and huge numbers, they deposit enormous amounts of feces, and when they die, their bodies decompose and foul the air. On Guam they covered the roads, and vehicles crushed so many that the roads became as slippery as ice.

Millions of dollars are spent every year by governments and

private planters to control the numbers of these snails. Poisons of various kinds and some species of parasitic flatworms have proven useful in the struggle. There is a small African snail called *Gonaxis* that eats *Achatina*. *Gonaxis* attacks mainly the younger snails, and even though these are still a good deal larger than *Gonaxis*, they fall victim. In attacking *Achatina*, *Gonaxis* cuts the muscle that pulls *Achatina* back into its shell. The giant snail is helpless because its main defense has been destroyed. *Gonaxis* clings fiercely and scrapes away with persistence until the larger animal is dead. Several years ago, large numbers of *Gonaxis* were imported into some Pacific islands where *Achatina* was troublesome. But in addition to eating *Achatina*, *Gonaxis* has an appetite for other smaller, harmless, interesting snails and has almost completely eliminated some species. So this method of controlling *Achatina* is not a very satisfactory one, especially from the point of view of animal conservation.

The shell of a giant African land snail, and the shell of one of its predators.

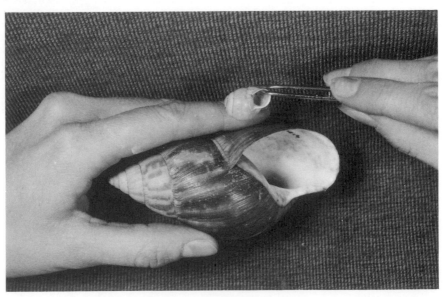

Achatina may be the largest and the worst, but there are other snails that are also extremely troublesome. They, too, devour seedlings and damage foliage and crops. In California there are several species that are particularly hated and for good reason. The fight against them costs time and money. Citrus crops, especially oranges, are sometimes damaged severely by snails, and biologists, farmers, and agricultural scientists are always searching for new, better, and more efficient ways of controlling pest snails.

SNAIL ENEMIES

The farmer has some allies in his fight against destructive snails. There are many animals that seem to like the taste of snails, among them birds, frogs, toads, squirrels, chipmunks, and many small forest creatures. Birds break snail shells by holding them in their beaks and smashing them against the sides of boulders. If you ever come across a boulder in a field with lots of freshly broken snail shells lying about, you can be sure that you have found such a "snail butcher shop." Squirrels bite off the tips of the shells to get to the meat inside. There are even some beetles in the family Cerambicidae (commonly called "long-horned" beetles) that eat pulmonate snails. The beetles have especially long mandibles so that they can reach into the shells for their prey. Land prosobranchs are attacked and eaten by the wormlike larvae of lightning bugs (fireflies). And, as we have seen, there are also cannibal snails. In many parts of the world, human beings, too, love snail tidbits.

The snail's worst enemy is probably weather. Icy winters and hot, dry summers can kill snails by the thousands. To cut such terrible losses, snails, like many other animals, slow up life processes such as heartbeat and breathing and go into a long, almost deathlike sleep. Snails that do this in winter are said to hibernate (*hiberno* is Latin for "winter"). Those that do it in summer are said to aestivate (*aestas* is Latin for "summer").

63

They become active again when the weather turns favorable. Perhaps, on a hot summer day, you will find a snail on your sidewalk or fence that has a shiny membrane across the opening of its shell. This snail is aestivating. An aestivating snail will often respond to the warmth and moisture of your hand by becoming active, popping its head and foot out of the shell and crawling around in your palm.

A handful of land snails from a New York City garden. An aestivation membrane can be seen across the mouth of one shell.

SNAIL DEFENSES

The best defense snails have is to keep out of sight. They search for food and mate mainly at night, hiding during the daylight hours. The shell does provide protection against smaller and weaker enemies. The land prosobranchs can hide behind their operculums, and some pulmonates produce lots of bubbly, sticky foam (mucus) to discourage enemies. Some snails grow a strong toothlike barrier just inside the opening of the shell. This is often as good as an operculum to keep foes from venturing in. Recently it was discovered that these barriers are covered with tiny bits of sharp shell that point outward. Hungry predators can't easily cross these prickly gates and have to look for a meal elsewhere.

THE SINGING SNAILS

In the mountains of Oahu in Hawaii live some of the loveliest land snails in the world. They are about as big as olives and are as brightly colored as flowers or butterflies. These snails live on the branches and trunks of trees and come to the ground only to lay their eggs. They are called "little agate snails" (*Achatinella*).

At one time these snails probably existed in the millions. A biologist who studied them in the nineteenth century reported that he could *hear* the snails from a distance. As numbers of them dragged their shells across the rough bark of the trees, the shells made a pleasant tinkling sound. From a distance, this sounded like gentle music. *Achatinella* was a singing snail.

In recent years, the numbers of these beautiful little agate snails have been sadly reduced. Overcollecting, land clearing, and cannibal snails introduced to control the giant African snail have all cut the number of *Achatinella* disastrously. But there is a strong movement afoot to save them from extinction. Even if successful, however, the tinkling sound of snail shells will probably never again be heard in the forests of Hawaii.

The Case of the Exploding Shell

A snail collector we know once received a package of land shells from New Zealand. Among them were several specimens of large, low shells about fifty millimeters (two inches) in diameter and about twelve millimeters (one-half inch) high. They were covered by a thick, strong, gleaming black outer skin, or periostracum, like patent leather, and there was a brilliant circular, rather wide yellow stripe on top. The snails are called *Paryphanta*; they are predatory snails from the mountains of New Zealand. The collector was pleased with this fine addition to his collection, made out a neat label, and deposited the shells in a drawer in his cabinet.

One night he was sitting at his desk working on his shell collection when he was startled to hear loud bangs coming from inside the cabinet. Alarmed, he jumped up and hastily began opening one drawer after another. There he found his beautiful *Paryphanta* shells in smithereens, as though someone had smashed them with a hammer. Only later did the disappointed shell collector learn what had happened.

The shell of *Paryphanta* is quite thin and fragile, but the shiny black periostracum is tough. When the shell is put into a dry place, the outer skin begins steadily to contract until it eventually forces the inner shell to collapse with a loud noise. In New Zealand, *Paryphanta* lives in mountain forests where rain is plentiful. Thus, the snail doesn't need to worry about its shell exploding.

6

Snails without Shells: Sea Slugs

On one of your visits to the public aquarium, perhaps you will be lucky enough to see, in one of the tanks, an unusually beautiful creature about five inches in length, exquisitely colored, with some tentaclelike structures in front. It will be swimming with a lovely, flowing motion, twisting and turning as though it were a beautiful dancer performing graceful movements. The animal is indeed commonly called the Spanish dancer, and believe it or not, it is a true mollusk. Sea slug may not be a pretty way to refer to this elegant creature, but a sea slug it is—a shell-less member of the opisthobranch (hindgiller) subclass of gastropods.

Shells, the snails' hard outer skeletons, have successfully protected these soft-bodied creatures for millions of years. In fact, biologists believe that the development of the shell was the most important feature in the evolutionary history of the phylum Mollusca. How then was it possible for some snails to lose their shells in the process of evolution without dying out? We will try to answer this question.

Throughout the long process of evolution, two large groups of snails lost their shells. One group became the land slugs; the

Top view of a sea slug (aeolid type).

other group became the sea slugs, all of which are placed in the subclass Opisthobranchia. Let us consider sea slugs.

One advantage conferred by the loss of the shell has been a modification of body shape over time. This permitted the sea slugs to adapt to their environments in new ways—to take on life styles, so to speak, which would have been impossible for snails burdened with heavy shells. The result of these evolutionary changes has been a wonderful variety of shapes, colors, sizes, and living habits. For example, there are sea slugs so tiny that they live in the spaces between the coarse sand grains of certain ocean beaches. As you can imagine, the bodies of such animals need to be very slender in order to squeeze through such small, irregular spaces. Although the sand grains continually shift and move around, the sea slugs live in the thin layer of seawater between the sand grains, where they gain some protection. Other tiny sea slugs live buried in sea sands in shallow bays and lagoons and eat the roots of seaweeds. There are sea hares, large thick, fleshy sea slugs, that glide lazily through meadows of sea grasses, grazing. In the open waters of tropical seas, tiny blue and white sea slugs drift with ocean currents and spend their lives safely feeding on the dangerous

Portuguese man-of-war jellyfish. Surprisingly, sea slugs are among the few animals that are able to feed on poisonous jellyfish without being killed by their stinging cells. On the sea bottom, different kinds of sea slugs have become adapted to feeding on many varieties of sea creatures, such as corals, sea fans, barnacles, sponges, moss animals, sea squirts, and others. Often these sea slugs have body colors which so perfectly match their prey that while sea slugs are feeding, they blend in with the background and are virtually invisible to potential enemies.

Having lost the protection of the gastropod shell, how do sea slugs protect themselves from enemies? Camouflage is probably the most common means of defense. Some sea slugs are so

Looking like a string of sausages, the egg mass of a sea slug is laid on a piece of seaweed. The honeycomb-like formation underneath is a colony of moss animals.

well protected by their colors or patterns that unless they are moving they simply can't be seen. But other clever defenses have evolved, too. Many sea slugs taste terrible on account of acid secretions and other chemicals that their skin produces. Whatever the styles of protection, they work. Sea slugs, although not as well known as some other marine animals, easily rank among the most successful, in spite of their vulnerable bodies.

The subclass Opisthobranchia contains a variety of distinctive groups of snails, not all of which are shell-less. Each of these distinctive groups is recognized by zoologists as a separate order. Three of these orders are largely or entirely without shells, and it is appropriate to term their members "sea slugs." The first of these orders is the group containing the sea hare.

Sea hares have been given the Latin name *Aplysia*, which comes from a Greek word meaning "dirty sponge." The original Greek meaning of the word *aplysia* may refer to the black, inky fluid that these animals produce when irritated or disturbed. In any case, the order to which the sea hares belong is called the *Aplysiomorpha*, where the *morpha* part means "shape" or "form."

Sea hares are large snails, reaching a foot in length and weighing up to two kilograms. Docile and slow moving, they are usually found in warm shallow seas where they graze on seaweeds. They are called sea hares because the two tentacle-like structures on their heads made people think of rabbit ears. Toward the rear of the animal are thick flaps, or "wings," one on each side, which beat slowly as this animal partly swims, partly crawls through beds of seaweed. When you first examine a sea hare, it appears completely shell-less. However, *Aplysia* has not entirely lost its shell. A small, thin, transparent remnant of the shell, about the size of a silver dollar, can be found partly enclosed within the skin of the back between the fleshy "wings."

Biomedical scientists have discovered that sea hares are very useful in certain kinds of experiments dealing with the function of nerves. The nerves of most animals are microscopic, and because of their small size and their location deep within the body, it is difficult to experiment with them. But the nerves of sea hares are so large they can be easily seen with the unaided eye. Since they are near the outside of the animal, they can easily be reached without seriously harming the sea hare. But because sea hares are not always common and cannot be collected at all times of the year, biologists encountered a problem working with them. Recently, however, they have learned how to grow sea hares in the laboratory. Adults are kept in aquariums and fed seaweeds; the eggs are collected and the larvae which hatch from the eggs are reared to adulthood—all in the laboratory.

The inky dye that sea hares produce when annoyed was once thought to be poisonous to humans. It isn't, but it does provide some protection for *Aplysia*, in just the way clouds of ink given off by a startled octopus confuse its enemies and permit it to escape unharmed.

Like every opisthobranch snail, each sea hare is both male and female (hermaphrodite). Once sea hares have paired off and fertilized their partner's eggs, each one separates and lays a large, folded or coiled ribbonlike egg mass containing hun-

Drawing of four mating sea hares forming a reproductive chain.

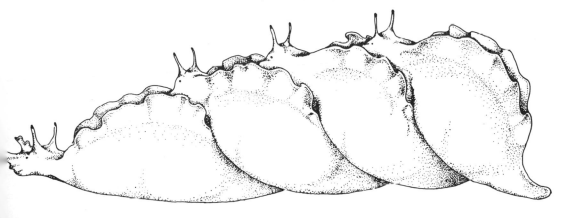

dreds of thousands of microscopic eggs. Each egg develops into a tiny, free-swimming veliger larva. For several weeks, these larvae drift in warm ocean currents, where they feed on microscopic phytoplankton cells. Eventually, the larvae settle on seaweeds on the ocean bottom. As the baby sea hares graze on the seaweed and grow, the shells becomes partly enclosed within the skin on the back of the animals and they are almost impossible to see from the outside.

The group of opisthobranchs that has attracted the most attention because of their beautiful colors and delicate shapes belongs to the order *Nudibranchia*, a word that means "naked gills"—that is, gills not hidden inside the body. The Spanish dancer is a member of the nudibranch order. Nudibranchs are most commonly found in shallow areas like reefs, rocks, wharfs, pilings, and breakwaters. All nudibranchs are completely shell-less as adults; but the nudibranch veliger larvae do have shells —very much like the shells of other marine snail larvae. When the nudibranch larvae settle to the bottom of the ocean, their tiny larval shells are discarded—actually cast off—and from that time until the nudibranchs die, they never again possess shells.

One group of nudibranchs has clusters of soft, fingerlike extensions covering the surface of their backs. These extensions resemble small, flexible horns and are named *cerata* after the Greek word for horn (*keras*). At the tip of each cerata, there is a small sac that contains stinging cells. The stinging cells are not produced by the nudibranch itself. Rather, they come from the bodies of sea anemones, corals, and jellyfish that the nudibranch has eaten. In a way that is not fully understood, they pass unexploded into the cerata of the nudibranch. When an enemy such as a fish approaches a nudibranch, the fingerlike cerata are turned toward the fish, as if inviting it to take a bite. If the fish bites off a bunch of cerata, the stinging cells discharge their poison into the mouth of one now rather surprised

An aeolid nudibranch on a strawberry hydroid. It will consume the entire mass of hydroid tentacles and "borrow" the stinging cells for its own cerata.

fish. It is a rare fish that returns for a second bite! Meanwhile, the nudibranch, which can easily grow a new cluster of cerata, has had time to escape. Sea slugs that possess cerata are called *aeolid nudibranchs* (suborder Aeolidiacea) in honor of the Greek god of the winds, Aeolus.

One species of aeolid nudibranch, *Glaucus*, spends its life drifting in the surface waters of tropical oceans. It can do so because it swallows a bubble of air from above the ocean's surface. The bubble is held in the stomach, where it provides the buoyancy that keeps the little animal from sinking. *Glaucus* feeds on the poisonous jellyfish called the Portuguese man-of-war. Hence the stinging cells in the cerata of *Glaucus*, which come originally from the jellyfish, are particularly bothersome. In Australia, winds sometimes drive large numbers of these tiny nudibranchs into shallow water near beaches, and swimmers rubbing against the nudibranch's cerata are stung by the stinging cells, just as if they had been attacked by the Portuguese man-of-war itself. But, of course, there are no jellyfish in sight. The fact that the sea slugs themselves are not harmed by the jellyfish poison is a mystery still not understood by marine biologists.

Another large group in the order Nudibranchia includes sea slugs with flat bodies covered by a leathery, fleshy skin. Near the rear end, each one of these carries a little circle of feathery gills. For some reason, these nudibranchs are called *dorid nudibranchs* (suborder Doridacea) in honor of Doris, the daughter of the Greek god Oceanus. Like other members of the nudibranch order, the dorids are fierce predators. They eat sponges, moss animals, soft corals, barnacles, and a multitude of other marine animals that grow as crusts on hard, underwater objects.

Dorid nudibranchs that eat sponges often become the exact color of the sponge on which they are feeding. By blending in with the sponge, the nudibranch is safe from the prying eyes of its foes. But the dorid nudibranch gains another advantage

from the sponge. Sponge tissue is full of sharp bits of limestone
—microscopic needlelike objects called *spicules*—and for this
reason is avoided by most fish. Thus, the dorid uses the sponge
for food, for camouflage, and for direct protection. Lucky
creature! But how is it possible for a soft-bodied animal like
a nudibranch to eat a sponge that is filled with needlelike spicules? Biologists are not sure, but probably the nudibranch coats

A dorid nudibranch. Note the circlet of gills on the sea slug's back.

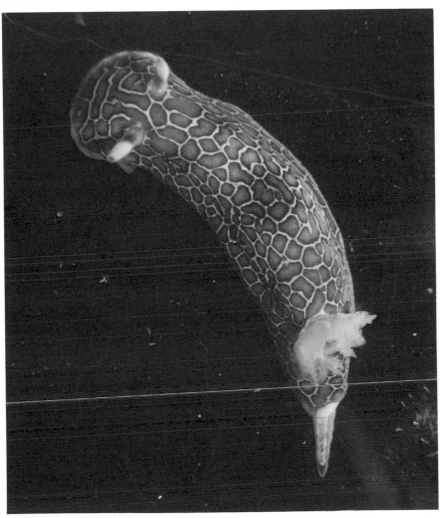

each mouthful with large masses of sticky mucus that then protects the inside of the nudibranch's digestive tract. Eventually the limestone spicules are broken up or dissolved in the nudibranch's stomach.

While some dorids are the same color as sponges or as other animals on which they feed, others have showy, bright-colored patterns. Biologists are somewhat puzzled by this. One explanation is that the colors actually advertise the nudibranch's presence as a warning to hungry predators, just as some poisonous snakes have showy patterns to warn enemies to stay away. We know that many dorid nudibranchs have glands in their skin that produce dangerous sulphuric acid. Thus, a fish or other predator that ignores the nudibranch's warning and takes a bite will have a very unpleasant experience, one it is not likely to repeat. One trouble with this theory, however, is that some highly colored nudibranchs live mostly under rocks and in crevices where little or no light penetrates, and they are virtually invisible to predators. The reason for bright colors in these species remains a mystery.

Another fascinating group of sea slugs feeds entirely on marine algae. The radulas of these snails consist of a single series of tiny hooklike teeth, which are used to pierce the cells of the algae, one cell at a time. Then the contents of each cell is sucked out, leaving only the outer cell wall of the algae. As the teeth on the radula wear out, they drop into a sac within the head of the sea slug, accumulating there throughout its lifetime. For this reason, sea slugs of this type are placed in the order *Ascoglossa*, meaning "sac of teeth."

Unlike the nudibranchs, some ascoglossan species still have a small, thin shell. The shell is always very fragile, and too small for the soft parts of the slug. The ascoglossans are common sea slugs, especially in shallow tropical waters, but are often overlooked because of their small size and their color,

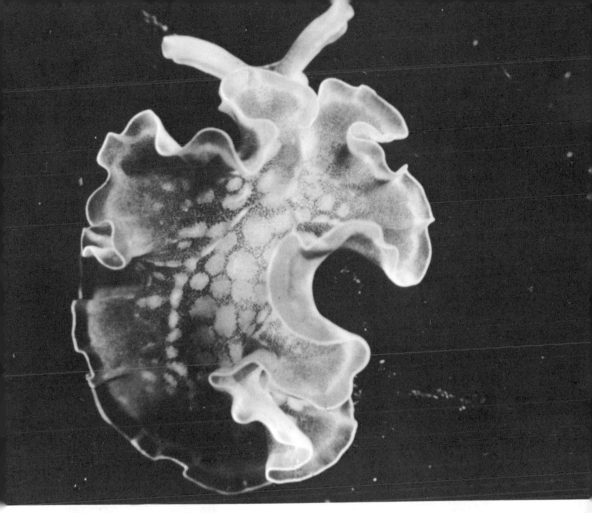

A shell-less Ascoglossan sea slug.

which usually matches the color of the plants on which they live and feed.

Some of the most unusual opisthobranch snails in the world are shelled ascoglossans. One of these was discovered for the first time in 1959 by a Japanese scientist who was so astonished by what he found that he hesitated a while before making it public. The tiny snail he discovered, now called *Berthelinia*, has a shell consisting of two parts, or valves, connected by a hinge. In other words, this snail has a bivalve shell! Until

Berthelinia was discovered, biologists had no idea that a snail could have a bivalve shell. These little snails have recently been found in many tropical areas, where they live nestled among certain kinds of marine algae. The bivalve shell of *Berthelinia* looks very much like a tiny clam shell. But *Berthelinia* is definitely an opistho-gastropod. At the outer part of the hinge connecting the two parts of the shell, there is a small, twisted spire—a sure sign that the bivalve shell originated from a single shell. Thus, each of these snails is born with one shell that divides into two parts as the animal develops.

Berthelinia, *the bivalve snail, crawling along a piece of seaweed, with its head extended down. The pattern on the skin of the mantle is visible through the transparent shell. In life, about five millimeters across.*

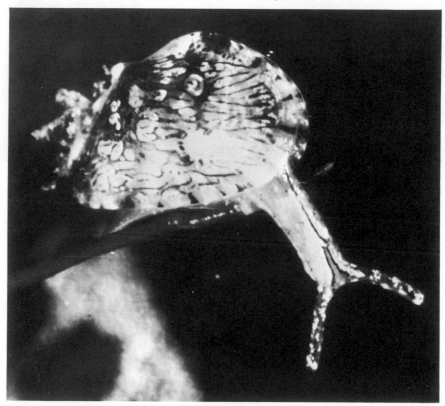

IMPORTANCE OF OPISTHOBRANCH SNAILS

Opisthobranch snails are of little direct use to man. However, they are among the sea's most startlingly beautiful creatures. In fact, in recent years, nudibranchs have become so popular among scuba divers and other marine biology enthusiasts that special clubs have been started for the express purpose of studying, photographing, and protecting nudibranchs. Of course, nudibranchs cannot be collected for their attractive shells—the beauty of a nudibranch is only "skin deep," and their colors quickly fade when preserved. But when captured on color film, their beauty lasts forever.

In addition to their beauty, some nudibranchs offer mankind utilitarian service. Nudibranchs are voracious predators and spend almost all of their time feeding. Because of this, some nudibranchs are important in reducing the fouling growth on pier pilings, ship's hulls, floating docks, lobster pots, and so on. Most of these fouling growths are caused by incrusting marine animals, such as barnacles, hydroids, moss animals, and sponges.

7
Land Slugs

Land slugs, like sea slugs, are also descended from snails with shells. Like the air-breathing land snails, slugs take in air through a breathing pore and breathe with a lung; and like most other snails, they use a radula for eating. In fact, the only difference between air-breathing land snails and land slugs is that, through evolution over thousands of years, the shells of the slugs have gradually disappeared. Of course, other changes in the bodies of slugs accompanied the loss of the shells. The visceral mass became flattened and sank down into the head and foot, and the body became almost perfectly bilaterally symmetrical. But why? Why did the shell disappear? How do land slugs benefit from these changes? Zoologists are not entirely certain, but some advantages have been suggested. The most obvious benefit is that snails without bulky, heavy shells are able to stretch their bodies so that they are thin enough to crawl through the narrowest of passages, even deep into the soil. Thus, slugs are able to escape the hot, drying rays of the sun by hiding in places that many snails could not enter. Another advantage the slugs gain by the loss of the shell is the possibility of living in locations where snails cannot. Snails need limestone (calcium) in order to build and repair their shells, and this calcium must come from the soil. Thus, snails are abundant where limestone is common, but scarce where limestone is absent—such as granitic and volcanic soils. But slugs do not need to worry about a supply of calcium. They live quite well in these places, so long as food and moisture are available.

But if these are some of the advantages of *not* having a shell, there are some disadvantages as well. The two main problems caused by not having a shell are the danger of drying out and the danger of being easily attacked by enemies. Land snails avoid losing body moisture by withdrawing into their shells and sealing off the shell entrance (aestivating). Slugs can't protect themselves this way. Their best escape is to crawl into narrow, damp spaces under rocks, boards, the bark of trees, and so on. This explains why slugs are most active at night, when it's damp, or just after rain. At these times, slugs can be active without drying out. If, however, a slug is exposed to dry air, it does have some ability to protect itself. By contracting its body so that it is only one-fifth or one-sixth the size it is when stretched out, a slug exposes much less surface area and therefore loses much less moisture. But even if a slug loses as much as half the water content of its body, it can still recover rapidly. One reason for this is that slugs absorb moisture through their skin. Unlike most other animals—such as human beings—they don't take in water only through the mouth.

The problem of protection from enemies is a major headache for slugs. For the most part, the best defense is to find a good hiding place. When slugs find a good place to hide, they often return to it every day. If they find a stranger occupying their favorite spot, they bite the intruder and try to drive it out. Thus, slugs are sure of having a permanent hiding place.

Many land slugs, like sea slugs, have a very unpleasant taste. These species are sometimes showy and colorful. The advantage of this is that a potential predator, such as a bird or mouse, can easily recognize and avoid a bad-tasting slug. Thus, the colorful advertisement slugs offer their predators keeps them from being eaten.

But how bad can a slug taste? A German writer once decided to find out. He ran his finger over the back of a very large slug and then put his slime-covered finger in his mouth. His reaction was immediate and violent. No matter how much he spit and rinsed his mouth, it was no use: the taste was still there. Even three glasses of whiskey, one after the other, didn't help. For three days after this experiment, he had no appetite for food. Sometimes young birds who have not yet learned about the bad taste of some slugs will attempt to eat one. The bird usually spits the slug out, then flutters about wildly and rubs its beak

A terrestrial slug. Note the eyes at the tips of the tentacles and the soil that has stuck to the mucus coating on the slug's body.

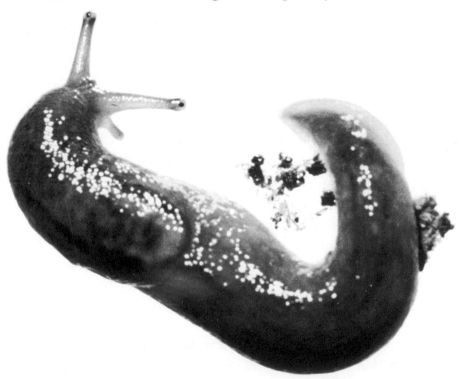

on the ground, as if trying to get rid of the bad taste. Even if the slug is killed in this encounter, the bird will have learned to avoid eating such slugs in the future. Many of these bad-tasting slugs are in the genus *Arion*. The foul taste of *Arion* slugs is probably caused by certain chemicals produced by the skin, along with the slime.

Not all slugs taste so terrible, and some of these are eaten by a variety of animals. Some slugs do what lizards do when attacked. They drop off a part of their foot, and it begins to twitch wildly. While the enemy's attention is diverted to the crazy moving part, the slug crawls away unharmed. It quickly grows a new portion of the foot in place of the old.

Thus we see that slugs can get along well without shells. In fact, members of many land snail families are gradually—through the process of evolution—turning into slugs. There are about five hundred species of land slugs known to science, but there are also about one thousand species of what Dr. Alan Solem, a well-known specialist, calls "semislugs." Semislugs are snails whose shells, already having become much smaller, are well on the way to disappearing altogether. As Dr. Solem writes, turning into slugs seems to be a popular trend among land snails. Clearly, the trend toward "sluggishness" is a successful one in nature. Ask any farmer or greenhouse owner, especially in the cool, moist climate of Europe or the northeastern part of the United States.

THE STICKY SLUG

Slugs have another defense against enemies. In Florida, the West Indies, and in many other warm parts of the world lives a very queer sort of slug. It is quite large, about ten to thirteen centimeters long (four to five inches) and about four centimeters wide (one and one-half inches) and looks something like a flat, narrow cookie. It has a smooth skin, no shell, and it is very sticky. Zoologists have named this slug *Veronicella,* and they believe that it is not closely related to most of the other slugs that we have been discussing. One reason for this view is that the tentacles of *Veronicella* do not turn inside out—as they do in most land snails—when they are pulled back inside the head. Instead, they collapse together, something like an old-fashioned telescope. But the tentacles are not the most remarkable thing about *Veronicella.* It is probably the stickiest creature in nature. One of the authors remembers the first sticky slug he ever saw. It looked so strange that he picked it up—and immediately wished he hadn't! The creature was sticky to begin with but seemed to give off even more slime the longer he held it. The sticky feeling stayed on his hand for days, and neither soap, alcohol, nor hard rubbing helped very much. He was more careful the next time he saw *Veronicella.*

WHAT SLUGS EAT

If you have ever had a garden, perhaps you have had the following experience. For a few days, the flower or vegetable seedlings you have planted are flourishing. Then one morning you find that the plants have large pieces chewed out of their leaves; some have even been eaten right down to the ground. The culprits are nowhere to be seen. In all likelihood, the culprits were slugs. Slugs can eat almost anything: dead animals (such as earthworms), decaying vegetables, and a wide variety of living plants. Unfortunately, slugs seem fond of crops—cereals, leaf and root vegetables, citrus and other fruits—the list of specific crops is very long.

Fighting slugs is expensive for farmers. There are poison pellets, poison sprays, special planting methods, and in some cases, plants that have been developed to resist slugs. Sometimes such plants produce chemicals that are distasteful or harmful to slugs.

84

In a garden, there is an easier way to control slugs. Slugs are attracted to beer. If you set out a few shallow dishes of beer in the evening, the slugs will be drawn to them and will drown in the beer. Although scientists cannot explain why slugs are attracted to beer (perhaps it is the yeasty odor), this is a useful method for controlling them and worth trying if you have a slug problem in your garden.

SLUG REPRODUCTION

Slugs reproduce in much the same fashion as terrestrial snails. All slugs are hermaphrodites and deposit their eggs in moist soil. While a slug may lay only twenty or thirty eggs at a time, a single individual may produce more than five hundred eggs during one season (slugs do not lay eggs during the winter). So you see, under favorable conditions, slug populations can grow very quickly.

Some slugs have peculiar and complicated mating rituals. Those of the large *Limax* slug are a good example. *Limax* is an immigrant, probably brought into the United States from Europe in flower pots or on plants. In any case, it is now common in city gardens and backyards. *Limax* reaches about ten centimeters (about four inches) when stretched out. When two slugs meet and prepare to mate, they begin to move slowly in a circle, tentacle to foot. The circle grows smaller and finally the slugs intertwine. Then, if the slugs are on a branch of a plant, they will crawl off and hang freely suspended in the air, each one attached to a strand of mucus anchored to the branch—like spiders hanging from strands of silk. There they remain for up to several hours. During this time, each slug fertilizes the other. Then, the slugs climb back up the mucus strands and crawl away. This curious mating behavior may be important to the slugs for the same reason that the darts are to the *Helix* snails. Since they are animals with relatively poor eyesight, this behavior helps the slugs recognize their proper

A slug, Limax, *with its newly laid eggs.*

partners, that is, individuals of the same species. This theory is largely guesswork, and there is still much to learn about the behavior and biology of slugs.

Land slugs are not very pleasant creatures in the eyes of most people; and, in fact, they seem to be positively repellent to many. But like all other creatures, slugs have their fascinating ways: how they eat, reproduce, defend themselves from enemies. And even if we don't find them as attractive as other snails, we must respect the way they are designed to overcome many obstacles in their environment, and the way they have become a very successful group of animals. While slugs create problems for farmers and gardeners, they are not dangerous to humans. They may be slimy and unpleasant to touch, but they won't bite, scratch, sting, or cause blisters. Slugs are perfectly safe to handle and study. Moreover, like all creatures, they have their value in the scheme of nature. Along with all other land snails, they contribute to the decomposition of plant matter, which is necessary to maintain the fertility of the soil. We hope that you may now feel a little more friendly toward these much misunderstood creatures.

Glossary

Achatina (a-cat-*tea*-na)—A large African snail that is a serious agricultural pest.

Achatinella (a-cat-tin-*ell*-a)—The colorful Hawaiian singing snail.

Aeolidiacea (ay-*oh*-lee-dee-*ace*-ee-a)—The suborder of nudibranchs that bear cerata.

aestivate (*ess*-ti-vate)—To pass the winter in deep sleep.

Ancylus (*ann*-si-luss)—A group of small freshwater limpets.

Aplysia (a-*plizz*-ee-a)—A large opisthobranch with a shell inside its body, commonly called a sea hare.

Aplysiomorpha—The suborder including the *Aplysia*.

apple snails—A group of often large freshwater snails that can breathe both air and water.

Archaeogastropoda (*ar*-kee-o-gas-tro-*po*-da)—The gastropod order that includes the most primitive snails.

Arion (*a*-ree-on)—A bitter, unpleasant tasting slug.

Ascoglossa (ass-co-*gloss*-a)—The suborder of nudibranchs that keep their discarded teeth in a special sac.

Berthelinia (ber-the-*lin*-ee-a)—The group of gastropods that develop a bivalve shell.

Bivalvia—The class of Mollusca with two shells: clams, oysters, and their relatives.

blood flukes—Parasitic worms that cause snail fever.

body whorl—The last, that is, the most recent, and usually the largest curved portion of a snail shell; it is the whorl nearest the foot.

brooding—The process of taking care of eggs before they hatch.

Cephalopoda (sef-a-la-*poe*-da)—The class of Mollusca including octopuses, squids, and their relatives.

Cerambicidae (ser-am-*biss*-i-dee)—A family of beetles with long jaws, which they use to reach into snail shells for their food.

cerata (ser-*ah*-ta)—The fleshy extensions on the backs of some nudibranchs.

cercaria (ser-*care*-ee-a)—The stage in the life cycle of the liver fluke that can enter the human body.

cilia (*sill*-ee-a)—Microscopic, hairlike, rhythmically beating structures found in many kinds of animals.

class—The division under phylum in the classification of the Animal Kingdom; for example, the class Gastropoda in the phylum Mollusca.

cone snails—Gastropods that produce beautiful, cone-shaped shells; their bites are often poisonous.

Doridacea (do-ri-*dace*-ee-a)—The suborder of nudibranchs with mainly smooth bodies. A circlet of gills surrounds the anus on the snail's back.

embryo—A stage of development; in the snail's life cycle, prior to hatching.

enzymes—Special chemicals produced by the body; they digest food and bring about other important chemical reactions.

Erminia desertorum (er-*min*-ee-a)—The desert snail that can survive years of uninterrupted hibernation.

fertilization—The union of a male sperm and a female egg that begins the process of embryo formation.

filament—A skinlike flap of tissue; filaments make up the gills of a snail.

Gastropoda (gas-tro-*po*-da or gas-*trop*-o-da)—The class of the phylum Mollusca that includes the snails.

giant African snail—see *Achatina*.

Glaucus (*glaw*-kus)—The nudibranch group that makes use of the stinging cells of the Portuguese man-of-war jellyfish.

Gonaxis (go-*nax*-is)—The group of snail cannibals that attack the giant African snail.

Helix (*hee*-licks)—A group of small land snails.

hermaphrodites (her-*ma*-fro-dites)—Creatures being male and female at the same time.

hibernate (*high*-ber-nate)—To pass the winter in a deep sleep.

Io (*eye*-oh)—A group of large, beautiful American freshwater snails, now endangered.

Limax (*lee*-max or *lie*-max)—A group of European land slugs introduced into the United States.

limpets—Gastropods that produce snail shells that look like Chinese hats or small cups.

liver rot—A serious disease of cattle caused by a parasitic fluke.

Lymnaea (limm-*nay*-a)—A group of freshwater pulmonate snails with shells opening to the right.

mantle—The thin inner tissue enclosing the body of mollusks.

mantle cavity—The space between the skirt of the mantle and the head of the gastropod.

Melampus (muh-*lam*-pus)—The pulmonate snails found in saltwater marshes.

Mollusca (mollusks)—The phylum of the Animal Kingdom including soft-bodied creatures, most of which produce an outer shell.

moon snails—A large family of burrowing marine snails with large round shells.

murex snails—see Muricidae.

Muricidae (mew-*riss*-i-dee)—A large family of marine snails that produce graceful and often very spiny shells.

mystery snails—see Viviparidae.

Nudibranchia (new-di-*brank*-ee-a)—An order of naked-gilled Opisthobranchia.

operculum (oh-*per*-kew-lum)—The horny (or shelly) lid or plate with which a snail can close off the mouth of its shell.

Opisthobranchia (oh-pisto-*brank*-ce-a)—The molluscan subclass that includes the snails having the gills behind the heart. This subclass includes all of the sea slugs.

order—The division in the classification of the Animal Kingdom that follows class; for example, the order Nudibranchia.

oyster drill—A small murex snail that eats young oysters.

Paryphanta (parr-cc-*fan*-ta)– The snail with the exploding shell.

phylum—The largest division in the classification of the Animal Kingdom; for example, the phylum Mollusca.

Physa (*fies*-a)—Freshwater snails with a low spire and large body whorl, also called tadpole snails.

phytoplankton (fie-toe-*plank*-ton)—Tiny drifting single-celled plants, the main food for some mollusks.

planarians—Flatworms, for example, the human blood fluke.

Pleuroceridae (ploo-roe-*ser*-i-dee)—A family of freshwater snails found mainly in southeastern United States.

pond snails—see *Lymnaea*.

proboscis—The snout possessed by many kinds of marine snails.

Prosobranchia (pro-so-*brank*-ee-a)—The molluscan subclass that includes the snails with their gills located in front of the heart.

Pulmonata (pull-mo-*nah*-ta)—The molluscan subclass of airbreathing snails.

radula—The ribbon of horny material embedded with rows of teeth, used for scraping food by mollusks.

rock snails—see Muricidae.

schistosomiasis (shiss-toe-so-*my*-a-sis)—A serious disease of human beings, also called snail fever, caused by a blood fluke that is transmitted by a snail.

sea hare—see *Aplysia*.

slipper limpet—The marine gastropod that changes its sex.

snail fever—see schistosomiasis.

Spanish dancer—Popular name for a very beautiful nudibranch.

spicules (*spi*-kewlz)—Tiny, sharp bits of hard calcium found in the skin of starfish and other marine creatures.

tadpole snail—see *Physa*.

trochophore (*tro*-ko-fore)—The first stage in the larval cycle of some primitive mollusks. The word means wheel-bearer and describes the shape of the creature.

Tulotoma magnifica (too-lo-*toe*-ma)—A group of beautiful freshwater mystery snails, now endangered.

veliger (*vell*-i-jer)—The snail larva that develops into a young snail.

Veronicella—A group of sticky slugs found in warmer parts of the world.

violet snail—A group of beautiful, purple snails that float on the surface of the water held up by their own bubble rafts.

visceral hump (*viss*-er-al)—The hump on the back of a snail, which contains the stomach, heart, kidney, and liver.

Viviparidae (vi-vi-*par*-i-dee)—A family of freshwater snails that give birth to live young.

wheel or ramshorn snails—A group of freshwater snails with a flattened coiled shell. They are called *Planorbus* and *Helisoma*.

Bibliography

Abbott, R. Tucker. *Kingdom of the Sea Shell.* New York: Crown Publishers, 1972. A beautifully illustrated full account of all sea mollusks in all their phases of study. Gastropods are emphasized.

Baker, Frank Collins. *Shells of Land and Water.* Chicago: A.W. Mumford, 1903. A charmingly written account of the life of all the mollusks, told in the form of the adventures of a teacher and his students. Recommended.

Burch, John B. *How to Know the Eastern Land Snails.* Dubuque, Iowa: W.C. Brown, 1962. A clear, useful guide to the identification of the land snails of North America east of the Mississippi. Only the scientific name of each species is given.

Hyman, Libbie H. *The Invertebrates*, Vol. VI; *Mollusca*, Vol. I. New York: McGraw-Hill, 1967. A very complete, technical account of the gastropods. Useful as a reference book for specific questions or for further study.

Rogers, Julie E. *The Shell Book.* Boston: C.T. Branford, 1951. A reprinting of the 1908 edition, with the names brought up to date, this deals with all classes of mollusks with many interesting chapters on land, freshwater, and marine snails. Recommended.

Runham, N.W. and Hunter, P.J. *Terrestrial Slugs.* London: Hutchinson University Press, 1970. A very thorough account of the biology, physiology, and the economic importance of land slugs. For advanced students.

Solem, G. Alan. *The Shell Makers.* New York: John Wiley & Sons, 1974. An introduction to mollusks for advanced students. Contains many excellent drawings and illustrations, some in color.

Tenney, Abby A. *Sea Shells and River Shells*. Boston, 1868. The first American children's book on the shapes and life habits of mollusks. Can be consulted in libraries.

Thompson, T.E. *The Opisthobranch Molluscs*. London: The Ray Society, 1976. A technical account of the subclass of gastropods containing the sea slugs. Beautifully illustrated with both line drawings and color photographs. While the text is for advanced students, the pictures can be enjoyed by all.

Index

NOTE: Numerals in italics refer to the captions of the illustrations.

Larvae, 31, 32, 38, 71, 72
Limax, 85, *86*
Limpet, 13, 23, 28, 37, 38, 46, 47
Liver fluke, 48
Liver rot, 48
Lymnaea, 45. *See also* Pond snails.

Malacologists, 9
Mantle, 22, 23, *78*
Mantle cavity, 23, 24, 40, 44, *45*, 46, 47, 53, 56
Maruzze, 7
Melampus, 51
Mollusca, mollusks, 10, 12, 13, 16, 67
Moon snails, 36
Mucus, *16*, 30, 65, 76, *82*, 85
Murex, 17. *See also* Rock snails.
Muricidae, 36. *See also* Rock snails.
Mystery snails, 41. *See also* Viviparidae.

Nudibranchia, nudibranchs, 72, 74, 76, 79. See also Sea slugs.

Operculum, 21, *24*, 25, 40, *43*, 44, 53, *54*, 55, 56, 65
Opisthobranchia, opisthobranchs, 25, *26*, 28, 38, 39, 67, 68, 70, 71, 72, 77, 78, 79
Orders, 70
Oyster drills, *36*

Paryphanta, 66
Penis, 31, 38
Phylum, 10, 67
Physa, 45. *See also* Tadpole snail.
Phytoplankton, 28, 31, 38, 72
Planarians, 48
Pleuroceridae, 41. *See also* Ribbed horn snails.
Pond snails, 45. See also *Lymnaea*.
Proboscis, *35*, 37
Prosobranchia, prosobranchs, *24*, 25,
30, 31, *33*, 38, 40, *42*, 44, 46, 47, *54*, 55, 56, 57, 58, 63, 65
Pulmonata, pulmonates, 44, 45, 46, 47, 51, 53, 54, 55, 56, 57, 58, 63

Radula, 28, *29*, 35, 37, 76, 80
Ramshorn snails, 45
Ribbed horn snails, 45. *See also* Pleuroceridae.

Schistosomiasis, 48, *49*, *50*. *See also* Snail fever.
Schnecken, 7
Sea hare, 68, 70, *71*, 72. See also *Aplysia*.
Sea slugs, *12*, 67, *68*, 69, 70, 74, 76. See also Nudibranchia.
Semislugs, 83
Siphons, 11, 23, *24*, *34*, *43*
Slugs (land), 10, 11, 12, 13, 15, 16, 17, 18, 53, 80, 81, *82*, 83, 84, 85, *86*, 87
Snail fever, 48. *See also* Schistosomiasis.
Spicules, 75, 76

Tadpole snails, *45*, 46, 51. See also *Physa*.
Trochophores, 30, 31
Tulotoma magnifica, *42*
Tyrian purple, 17

Veliger, 31, 32, 38, 58, 72
Velum, 31
Veronicella, 84
Violet snail, 28
Viscera, 21
Visceral hump, 21, 22, 25, 80
Vishnu, 18
Viviparidae, viviparid, 41, 42. *See also* Mystery snails.

Wheel snails, 45
Whelk, *34*, 35

4